Celeste VanFill

Grace Upon
Amazing Grace

Jackie,
We don't know each other very well — but I do know that the Lord is our constant and our Hope, in all things and through all things. Thank you for using your gifts to praise His name. May swift healing come your way and know His Grace is always sufficient!

Grace Upon Amazing Grace

A Memoir of Surviving Grief, Encountering Divine Appointments, and Living with an Eternal Perspective

Coleene VanTilburg

ABUNDANT HARVEST
PUBLISHING

Editing/Formatting: McKenna Hafner/Erik V. Sahakian
Cover Design/Layout: Andrew Enos
Back cover photo: Nicole Liebgott

Scripture quotations taken from the New American
Standard Bible ® (NASB), Copyright © 1960, 1962, 1963,
1968, 1971, 1972, 1973, 1975, 1977, 1995 by The
Lockman Foundation. Used by permission.
www.Lockman.org

Library of Congress Control Number: 2020916917

ISBN 978-1-7349949-2-6
First Printing: September 2020

FOR INFORMATION CONTACT:

Abundant Harvest Publishing
35145 Oak Glen Rd
Yucaipa, CA 92399
www.abundantharvestpublishing.com

Printed in the United States of America

This book is dedicated to the memory of my son, Timothy, and to my husband, Ted, and youngest son, Corey—all for God's eternal glory...

Contents

Foreword

I do not believe in coincidence. I accept that God is in control and that the Holy Spirit leads us in the direction to perfect God's plan for our lives and His world. Given this premise, I want to share with you the story of how *Grace Upon Amazing Grace* came into being.

Over fifteen years ago, my closest friend, Cathy, told me of another friend of hers who was struggling with all the severe aftereffects of a house fire. She told me the family chose not to move back into their home. Instead, they squeezed into an apartment that was too small for the couple, their two adult sons, and their dog, Chance. Everything in their lives had been upended and scattered with ashes and tears. I felt badly for them but didn't know what to do to help.

Over the following months, Cathy apprised me of how this family was doing. She wanted the two of us to meet and invited Coleene to come and attend our small prayer and praise group. When I met her, I felt an immediate affinity for her. She shared with me how her older son had severe kidney disease and fought both anxiety and issues with pain management. I also have spent a lifetime battling digestive disease and felt for Tim's struggles.

Cathy had seen my writing from earlier in my life and wanted me to take up my craft and begin to write again. I resisted mightily, but she continued to come up with reason after reason about why I should start again. I felt betrayed by writing and no longer trusted anyone with seeing my innermost thoughts typed out on a page.

However, Coleene poured forth writing. Cathy wanted me to do the same and felt she needed to connect us for both of our benefits. Cathy is a pretty smart lady and a very good friend; and she is nothing if not persistent.

Month after month passed. We continued to praise God together and plead for both Tim and my health to improve. In December of 2006, I was hospitalized at Christmas and things only got worse once I returned home. I no longer had the energy to go to our group and learned through another mutual friend that Tim had died the following February. Micki asked me to bake dessert for Tim's memorial service. I happily baked the brownies but did not attend the service. Given my current health issues, Tim's death hit a bit too close to my own circumstances.

My brother and his wife correctly realized that some of my health issues stemmed from the duplex we rented that had black mold. They showed us a condo they wanted to invest in for us to rent. We spent the next seven months preparing for the move and I lost track of how Coleene and Ted were coping with the death of their son. However, Cathy delivered a colorful monthly newsletter that Coleene wrote. Meanwhile, I began writing for the FaithWriters' weekly challenge, just as Cathy had hoped.

Within weeks of us moving into the brand new condo, not only was I feeling much better, but Gary's arthritis improved as well. We both knew that we had been living in a sick house—the mold affected our health that much. As soon as

I felt better, I decided to start volunteering in our church office. Coleene worked at a nearby high school and sometimes I had the chance to drive her home after we both finished our work for the day. We renewed our connection and spent many afternoons happily sharing our writing and praying together. We found a connection through writing. It provided catharsis for Coleene and helped me stop squandering the gift God gave me.

By the spring of 2009, I completed a Bible study and my membership at our church. In the final segment of the study the moderator challenged us to take what we had learned and apply it to a ministry. The moment he said it, I knew I wanted to start a Christian writers' group. Help would be required with this endeavor and Coleene would be the perfect coleader in my estimation. At our next praise and prayer meeting, I bubbled over with excitement about this idea and wondered what my friends—and most importantly, Coleene—thought of this idea. I received lots of support but could tell that Coleene had some reservations. However, she too encouraged me to continue developing the idea.

By the fall, everything was prepared. We planned to co-lead the Aspiring Writers' Forum (AWF). We both felt strong direction from the Holy Spirit to take this path and walk together. We felt scared but determined to follow through with the plan to the best of our abilities. Coleene's family still struggled with the financial impact of the fire and the recession. So, my husband, Gary, and I picked her up at her house before our meetings and drove her home afterward. Riding together gave us the opportunity to discuss how our group was growing and thriving, and to talk about what we were working on with our blogs and other writing.

By journaling together in the Aspiring Writers' Forum, we gained insight into one another and grew closer with our many shared interests. The Lord continued blessing our efforts. At the end of our second year working together, I began thinking that Coleene had an important book to write. I wanted her to tell the story of how she relied on God to help and support her in grieving her son. Many times, we spoke of miracles God showed us in everyday life. Sometimes we texted about swallowtail butterflies, or how we had seen someone running backward, or how a gift landed on our doorstep from an unknown person. We trusted one another in sharing the smallest of things we saw as grace miracles. We trusted one another with our writing and that we would honor God always with our words.

One night in May, Gary drove us home after AWF. We stopped to fill up with gas and I kept feeling prompted to tell Coleene about how important I thought it was for her to write a book about Tim and his life and death, and how God was working in her family. Coleene said she would pray and think about it.

I have attempted to write a memoir and know how much pain it unearths in the process. I have sat in front of the computer trying to type, unable to see a thing through the curtain of tears closing off my sight. By the time school finished for that summer, Coleene had three months to work on her project. She pulled out her journals, newsletters, poetry, and I don't know how many Bibles. Many summer days she brewed her pot of coffee, turned on her music, opened the Word, and began writing.

She amazed me with the innovative approach she took. Because she loves and relies upon music, along with her husband Ted, she compiled playlists of songs that they used to cope with their grief. Anywhere in a chapter, verses from the Bible supported what she wrote in her narrative and prayers frequently ended it. Poems that she had written at the time sprouted anywhere in the text. Every word she wrote was read first to AWF for critique and comment. The group encouraged her through our tears.

When she finished writing she chose several trusted friends to read her completed manuscript and began the arduous process of rewriting. Our worship director, Robbie, gave her especially constructive advice because he didn't know anything about Tim and all the family had gone through. A newcomer to our church, he spotted the areas where an average reader might get lost. Coleene took all this advice and counsel, and pressed in using all of it to strengthen her writing and her book.

Last summer I asked Coleene if she was ready for me to read through her book in total and line edit as well as copyedit it. I picked up her just printed manuscript on the weekend of the Fourth of July. I thought I would get it back to her within a few weeks, but trying to be a good editor while working on the memoir of a special friend proved to take a bit longer. I spread her manuscript out on my desk, pen in hand, sticky notes at the ready. I don't think I finished up the work until mid-September. I placed a sticky note prominently on her title page, telling her what an honor it was for me to walk alongside her on this journey.

In summary, remember to trust the Lord and look for the good in any given difficult circumstance. We have learned together after partnering for years that the Lord has a wonderful journey for all of us, if we simply trust Him and let Him lead the way. May your journey be blessed with love, laughter, and spiritual growth directed by the Holy Spirit.

Sincerely,

Linda Boutin

Prelude

I traced the vertical scar across my abdomen with my finger; it was a reminder of an entryway into this world, as well as an exit from the womb. A couple of decades later, I held out my hand to his scar as it undulated down his chest. Grotesque, purple and red, swollen and draining... The hands of the skilled tried to bind back up that which they had splayed open. My exit wound still remained, but deeper wounds laid beneath the surface. I knew of only one who truly healed. I knew Him, and He and I began to make divine appointments.

~~~

Notebooks, plain and fancy journals, the backs of envelopes... I've even been known to write things on the palms of my hands at times. There is something in me that causes me to think beyond and to look further. It causes me to keep a thought or picture of something and discover more about it. I think it is part of the artist in me. As an avid reader, books have always stirred my imagination, especially when I was a child.

I learned quickly that journaling isn't always easy when you are trying to raise a family of two busy boys and their equally active dad. Occasionally, I gripped a pencil and jotted down some thoughts, documented some achievements, scribbled some silly rhymes, and captured some great notes. Yet, a journal was never a consistent fixture in my life until I needed it to be, for my own peace of mind, for spiritual conversation, and for prayers and revelations.

I wrote it all down—pleading words, questioning words, surrendering words, transparent words. I was grateful that I found myself filled again from writing. I wrote it all down because I experienced it, and only then could the reflection and prayer over such words be rewarded in eternal intimacy.

It is also important for anyone reading this to know that music moves me. I love song lyrics, and the passions of verse and chord, but I vehemently deny that I can carry any tune or play any instrument. You might've seen me before; I am the one rocking out at the stop sign, and the one busting out in full vocals at the intersection…with the car windows tightly sealed, of course. I am also a firm believer that several songs played together can tell a story.

"Where words fail, music speaks."
— Hans Christian Andersen

In this memoir, I will pull from journal entries, memories, and younger and more hopeful days. Some words were written in the midst of a forceful gale, resulting in several pages of deep, raw emotion. Other pages came about slowly, like a sweet, gentle breeze that lingers until the words are just right. I have experienced blustery days, as well as days of silence and stillness. Even in the stillness, I felt "The Breath." We may never see it, but we can see what it touches and what it moves.

Every day I am inspired by the special needs kids I work with; I jotted down this conversation I had with a student one day. I've learned that some can see more than they are able to express. It made me smile to know that my student saw something more, something deeper, and something notable. He saw something worth remembering in me.

"When I think about you, I can see you sitting on your knees at night and praying," he told me.

"Well, that's a nice thought. What made you think of that?"

"Because I know you like religion and God stuff."

"I like to think of myself as more spiritual than religious."

After a thoughtful pause, he asked, "What's the difference?"

"My connection to God is always with me," I tried to explain. "I don't have to be in a church; I can feel Him now."

"Just like butterflies!" he replied.

Chapter 1

November 2003

Another day, another November… I got ready for work in between getting some chores started. My sons, now older and slightly more independent, headed their separate ways. Corey, a senior in high school, had a late start schedule that morning. I noticed him up and moving, but not too enthused; he wasn't a morning person. My other son, Tim, who is five years older than Corey, had already departed to meet a friend.

It was the Tuesday before Thanksgiving, but I didn't have much on my mind that morning other than the previous weekend's laundry, which seemed to be multiplying by the hour. My thoughts briefly flickered to the past; it had been three years since my mom, in the early hours of Thanksgiving morning, ushered her broken heart up to Jesus. While she feasted with Him in heaven, feelings burned inside of me; my heart still missed her terribly. My dad had also died in November, 21 years ago and just one week before Thanksgiving. He had only enjoyed two short years on earth with his first grandson, Tim.

Before heading out the door, I checked in with Corey. He had found the TV in Tim's room and made himself comfortable…*not* getting ready for school. "Be ready when Rodney gets here. You can't miss school," I told him before hauling two loads of laundry out to the garage. A strong wind blew in from the canyon against the house.

Of course, a Santa Ana and it's in the eighties outside, I thought irritably.

Thoughts of thankfulness, frosted pumpkins, and falling leaves seemed elusive, mostly because I just didn't want to make the effort. A sudden gust whipped and whistled, shaking the house and stirring me back to my routine.

I arrived at work for my usual shift—9:00 AM to 5:30 PM. Less than an hour in, my supervisor rushed over to me. "Pick up the phone," she said, "It's an emergency!"

My neighbor, Connie, was on the other end. "Coleene, honey, your house is on fire. Get home! Corey and the dog are okay!"

I looked up, stunned. I think I heard my boss say, "Go, just go! We'll take care of everything here!"

I immediately ran to my locker and gathered my things. As I ran out the door, I saw it—the smoke—thick and heavy, rising from the east where my house sat less than a mile away.

I owned a fast car and that day I used it to its full potential. My house was four streets away. As I approached, I saw barriers set up in the road. A policeman met my panicked glance.

He started to say something like, "Ma'am, you can't—"

"That's my house!" I yelled before he could finish,

adding a few words I regretted saying later.

I spotted Corey with the dog. He stood with my neighbor, tears streaming down his face. I pulled him into a long embrace. A fire engine and other emergency vehicles surrounded my property. I ran toward the house and saw the garage completely engulfed in flames; the winds from both the fire and the Santa Anas whipped hot. My new windows were smashed and broken, and "the best garage door on the street" rippled up like a Japanese fan.

I inquired with a fireman about my cat. He flagged down one of his crewmembers to look for her. He began to inform me all that they were doing to fight the fire—venting the ceilings, covering the furniture with a thick plastic, and shutting off the power.

I remember the heat.

I recall the smell.

Puff, my cat, was cradled in the arms of the fireman; he had found her under my bed. He held an oxygen mask to her face. Her whiskers protruded from the mask as her little heart thumped out of her chest.

Meanwhile, I paced. I made calls. I got angry when stupid people, looky-loos, and opportunists butted in. One fireman told me he'd never seen anybody handle insurance adjusters like I did. Eventually, people from Red Cross arrived. I called my husband, who worked over two hours away; he didn't quite believe the extent of the damage until he arrived.

With the fire finally quenched, I sat on the brick planter, wilted roses behind me. Finally, all the pain I'd been holding in started to release as the fear of what came next soaked in. My neighbors loved me and did what good neighbors do— made calls to help us out. I thought again of the month of November and the Thanksgiving holiday. Later that day, when I left the property, I knew I only needed two things: my Bible and a notebook. The realization stirred an ever-so-slight feeling of thanksgiving in my heart; despite the ashes that covered it, God's Word remained.

After 24 years in that house, memories etched themselves in the walls, echoed down the halls, sat atop the nightstands, and gathered around the dinner table. A million questions swirled in my head… What was I going to hold on to? What would I have to let go? What new changes were ahead? What was the restoration process going to look like? Would we, as a family, survive this? Is this from You, God?

For the next five years, I dwelled in a "cave," attempting to respond to the personal emergency within my own soul. I put on my fire protection gear, vented a few ceilings, and tried to secure my heart.

However, the ashes remained, and fire can stoke up again when the winds of this world blow hot and strong.

PLAYLIST I

Fire and Ash

1. "Against the Wind" — Bob Seger & The Silver Bullet Band
2. "Safe & Sound" — Taylor Swift
3. "If The House Burns Down Tonight" — Switchfoot
4. "From the Ashes" — Martina McBride
5. "The Spark" — Tenth Avenue North
6. "Consuming Fire" — Third Day
7. "Start A Fire" — Unspoken
8. "Held" — Natalie Grant
9. "HARD LOVE" — NEEDTOBREATHE
10. "Diamonds" — Hawk Nelson
11. "I Have This Hope" — Tenth Avenue North
12. "Remain" — Royal Tailor
13. "Something in the Water" — Carrie Underwood
14. "Broken Things" — Matthew West
15. "My Revival" — Lauren Daigle
16. "Even If" — MercyMe

Chapter 2

September 1980
(We Have A Son!)

Ted and I got married in 1977 and bought our first home two years later. That year, the Santa Ana winds lasted from the late summer until the early spring. They howled down through the valley and hit us midway before blowing over into Orange County. Our house was situated in the western part of the Inland Empire of San Bernardino County, California. We planted our roots in "cow country," otherwise known as a growing town called Chino. The only thing under our foundation was the distant memory of a walnut tree grove.

As I tell this story, the Santa Ana winds seem to be a formidable partaker. I recall another wind-whipped day in September—one where pain, joy, and pride rose to warm me, burning an eternal place in my heart. It was early fall in the year 1980. As a warm Santa Ana blew, my belly tumbled, preparing to give birth to a whirlwind of changes in our life.

Timothy Brian VanTilburg emerged into the world by C-section after a long night of waiting, worrying, anticipating, and getting x-rays. Sliced open from the naval down, I rested in recovery after receiving anesthesia. I struggled to wake up. It seemed like forever before I set my eyes on our sweet newborn.

"Perfect!"

"Beautiful!"

"So cute!"

The words spilled out from everybody's lips—Ted, my parents, my sister, Ted's parents. All of them had seen our baby boy before I did.

Across the room, my parents were relieved after recalling a flashback from my childhood. At only four years old, I was brought to the hospital for eye surgery. Unbeknownst to my parents and the doctors, I was allergic to sodium pentothal, and I violently convulsed after consuming it for the surgery. Two doctors had to hold me down while another found a remedy. Now, some 22 years later, my proud and tearful mother, now a *grandmother*, sighed in relief at the sight of her first grandchild.

The nurse handed me a 7-pound, 14-ounce, 19½-inch bundle. He was swaddled tight and smelled of newborn sweetness. We bonded immediately. I unwrapped him carefully and counted all of his tiny fingers and touched his little toes, soaking up the precious gift of love. I hugged him close, his own beating heart pressed against mine.

I couldn't believe we had a son! I wanted nothing more than to have a son first, for my dad whose days were drawing to a close, for my husband who was a sports guy, and for myself to love and teach.

Boys are fun. They play "rough and tumble," they are

messy, and they don't need to be perfect. Full of competitiveness and drive, inquisitiveness and passion, boys learned their lessons through scrapes and bruises. That is how my dad, a man self-taught in many skills, learned so much; the same could be said of Ted's dad. Our son, Timothy Brian—or Timmy, as he was soon nicknamed— had the advantage of learning from his two strong grandfathers and his own dad.

I looked at my beautiful son and thought of a thousand questions. What did God have planned for his life? Would I be the mom he needed? Would he grow up to love and respect me? Will he know how loved and cherished he is by his family, as well as by the God who goes before him?

For me, as a new mom, everything seemed perfect. I had an amazing husband and together we had a beautiful son, an adorable dog, and a nice home. I knew the blessing of my life at that moment.

Eventually, Timmy's bald head grew blond—almost white—with locks from his Dutch heritage. Active and smart, he kept me more than busy. He also spent the most precious times with his dad, taking bubble baths, washing the dog and cars, running around the beach, and canoeing. As the first grandchild on both sides of the family, Timmy certainly made his mark on the family tree. His cousin, Kevin, would arrive just a month later.

After a few years, Ted and I considered the possibility of growing our little family. We thought it was time for Timmy to have a brother or sister and learn the hard truth that he wasn't the center of the universe. In 1984, fall brought with it an Indian summer. The winds constantly whistled outside our windows, causing our allergies to flare up with intensity.

One morning in particular, Timmy woke up with his eyes swollen shut. His eyelids looked as thin and puffy as a water balloon. I punched in the numbers for his doctor and made an appointment for the same day. Dr. Ibrahim examined Timmy and prescribed him allergy medication with instructions to follow up in a week. A few days later, I was dialing the doctor's number again. Timmy's stomach was now bloated and the skin around his legs was tight— certainly not signs of ordinary allergies. I held him close to me, wishing I could take away his pain. More than anything, I wanted answers to what was plaguing my son.

On one particular visit, Dr. Ibrahim handed Timmy a little cup to pee in, which was extremely funny to my son. Timmy always had a charming personality, even when he wasn't feeling too great.

We'd only been home for an hour when Dr. Ibrahim called me back, having received the test results. I answered the phone, not knowing the news I'd receive would completely change our lives. Dr. Ibrahim expressed his concerns and gave us very specific instructions. We were to return to the San Antonio Regional Hospital Emergency Room in Upland and check Timmy in. I remember only a few key phrases from that phone call, such as "kidney trouble," "inflammation," and "retaining fluids." Tears flooded down my face as fear settled against my chest. My hands shook as I dialed my mom's number, then my neighbor, Joyce's, after. I eventually got ahold of Ted, who was busy at a construction site. He quickly drove home and we rushed around the house. I grabbed Timmy, as well as his favorite blanket, and we headed up Mountain Avenue to meet Dr. Ibrahim.

As the doctor informed us of what chronic kidney disease entailed—the physical end of it, mainly—we understood that a hard emotional and spiritual journey sat ahead of us. The real "rough and tumble" days were still to come. Winds of uncertainty whistled and knocked against the hospital window, simultaneously whipping against the foothills of my own heart.

I prayed, "Lord, be our strength."

Chapter 3

Growth

By the following spring, I was pregnant. The due date appeared to coincide with the holidays—a Christmas baby! Timmy started kindergarten and every day I waddled up the street with him in tow to his classroom at Alicia Cortez Elementary School.

I will never forget his first official day of school. Timmy made a dramatic debut, wrapping himself around my legs as I tried to leave. He cried as if my "abandonment" was torture. Eventually, he warmed up to the idea of spending all day at school. His teachers described him as precocious, talkative, attention-demanding, but also very smart.

Since Timmy was born in late September, Ted and I were presented with the option to hold him back for a year in order to give him a chance to mature. After receiving counseling and advice about it, we decided to move him on to the next grade. You know what they say… "Hindsight is 20/20."

I sat on the couch, very pregnant, with Timmy snuggled up beside me. He reached up to my face and turned it toward him. He liked to do that to make sure he had my full attention. Then he asked, "Does the baby have Jesus in his heart?"

I was shocked. How could I answer that question in a way my 4-year-old could grasp? Also, why was my 4-year-old asking me such a profound, spiritual question?

"Yes," I said. "There is a place where God lives in a baby's heart. When the baby gets older and can talk like you do, he or she will know Jesus loves them too, just like you do."

"He's a brother," Timmy announced, "And I will tell him."

Corey Patrick, my second son and Timmy's younger brother, came into this world on December 26, 1985. No anesthesia would keep me from seeing my precious newborn this time. Like his brother, Corey was delivered by C-section, along with an epidural and the strange sensation of tugging and pressure. Nevertheless, Corey came out healthy and hungry. Unlike with Timmy, my dad wasn't there to greet my second son; he had passed away in 1982.

Tim talked—to his brother, to his parents, to anyone and everyone. He talked all the time and everywhere. He talked to us, over us, and for us. Corey tried to keep up with his older brother by pointing and grunting. Eventually, I grew concerned over Corey's lack of verbal communication. I took him to the doctor to check his hearing. The doctor, aware of Timmy's talkative nature, asked me how much he communicated for his baby brother. I had to admit…it was a lot.

After that appointment, we began attempts to quiet a little man-child so that his baby brother had a chance to form his own voice, vocabulary, perspective, and point of view. Thus, the grace began.

Chapter 4

Life

We did life.

Grandma Joyce skied down the bunny slope with Timmy. Invitations arrived in the mail for the birthday parties of cousins and classmates. Sand, transferred from every beach in California, piled in the backseat of our car from weekend canoeing races. I sewed costumes for the kids every Halloween and recycled them—a lion, a clown, a pirate. The boys stood on the deck of the high school pool, at first shivering and nervous, but before long doing cannon balls off the high dive. Cub Scout meetings gathered the pack on Tuesdays, and Awana kept Corey busy on Wednesdays. Stacks of homework and notes were piled high on the dinner table. Cookie dough stuck to my sons' faces as they licked the beaters. We rocked out to music on the radio and, in quieter times, memorized Bible verses as a family. We had a dog to love and eventually say goodbye to, and another that adopted us. We even took a couple of memorable road and camping trips along the way. Tiny Tots, gymnastics, tee-ball, minor league baseball games, and soccer filled our calendar throughout those growing years.

In between it all, Timmy suffered relapses of his kidney disease—nephrotic syndrome. It showed up every other month, lasting about ten days each time. Those days were spent at home, of course, missing school and returning to the high doses of anti-inflammatory drugs. Eventually, he'd go back to school and the cycle would continue, over and over and over again. Anxiety plagued my oldest son, rearing its debilitating head. He'd often pick at a spot of hair on his head, twisting and pulling at it until he had a quarter-size bald spot. Once one anxious tick disappeared, another would take its place.

School also started to become a challenge for him. What he could not control—his exuberant need to talk, inform, entertain, and make people laugh—became his charming default. After a stint of missing school, Timmy liked to remind everyone in his characteristically dramatic way that he was back. This was not always appreciated by his teachers. Calls from the assistant principal's office came quite frequently. Once again, I consulted Timmy's doctor about his hyperactivity; however, the doctor remained adamantly against the drugs that were believed to help hyperactivity due to the large amount of medicine Timmy was already taking for his kidneys.

~~~

The blanket hung from his clutched fist. He held it under his nose so he could smell it and feel it against his face. Once bright yellow, it had since turned to a dingy, grayish reminder of yellow, and it was now much thinner. Nevertheless, that special blanket accompanied Timmy almost everywhere for a number of years. He held it especially close when he was feeling sick or needing to calm down. As he got older, the clinging lessened, realizing how the action might appear outside of his home. Once again, I asked his doctor about it and read up on security blankets. Most of the research told me that they were good things, a sort of cure and coping mechanism used to fight against anxiety and hyperactivity.

While his brother struggled with bouts of sickness, Corey, now very capable of speaking for himself, showed an independence he learned from his brother. When school started for Corey, he was out the door without so much as a blink.

"Bye, Mom."

"Oh, no… You're not walking to school by yourself," I told him.

Corey played hard and feared nothing. Whereas Timmy was impulsive about a lot of things, he didn't take the risks Corey did. Because I didn't get to experience the dynamic of brothers when I was a child, I hoped for my sons to be close as the years went by. Indeed, they loved on each other, protected each other, told on each other, and fought with each other. While Timmy persevered with words, Corey dominated in physical power. They collaborated outside, doing what boys do—digging holes, exploring the wash, riding bikes, skating up and down the street, chasing the dog, stepping in stuff, sneaking snacks, and competing at card games. They even travelled to their Oma and Opa's house up north on a plane…by themselves. They also went to Sunday school and church camps together.

In between it all, again, Tim got sick. His eyes puffed up and his stomach bloated out. He experienced everything from ravaging hunger to lethargy, pitting edema to emaciation. The cycle of steroids he was prescribed continued to fill his daily diet. So began the stages of his illness, this chronic, horrible condition.

~~~

Timmy took the blanket and held it under his nose. Soft, comforting, reassuring... Somehow this was grace. It was something he needed. His little blanket had so many holes and snags, compromises and imperfections, yet it was full of so much love. That blanket was a gift of grace that my son needed. Though he tossed it on the floor of his room or wadded it in the back seat of the car, and even though it seemed to shrink over time, its purpose never faded. He never outgrew it.

He often searched for it when he was older, long past the age that requires a safety blanket, but it brought him peace, it brought him calm, and it brought him love. It comforted him and listened to him. We would search the house from top to bottom to find that blanket, but the search never lasted long. We would soon discover that what we needed was never lost. We were the ones that moved. The blanket never grew feet and walked away. It simply waited until he was ready to receive its love and comfort again. It waited for him to humble himself and cuddle up in the grace it had to offer. He'd smell the peace wafting from it into his nose, finding the assurance that everything would be okay.

Life wrapped in grace... Isn't it all so amazing?

Chapter 5

The Need for a Fire

Destroyed… No longer in existence… Only memories remain…

A once recognizable form, it was now liquefied, melted, and morphed into a hardened blob of whatever. Things were stuck to each other and became like a mixed soup of leftovers. The colors were muted from the ash, dulling the original intent. A wooden beam that once held the structure in place now sat diagonal, its two-by-fours exposed like the ribs of a carcass. Another fallen crossbeam created an "X," indicating that this place had been deleted, the lives that once dwelled here no longer welcome back. The yellow caution tape mimicked the same form. Black scars marked the travel of the fire.

What good could come from this?

In this situation, "nothing" seemed like the obvious answer.

My mind, flooded with emotions, was drawn to the picture of a forest fire. When a fire breaks out in the wilderness, most of the time it was started by a lightning spark. The old growth and decayed trees which line the forest floor provide the perfect kindling for destruction. The fire burns through leaves, logs, pine needles, and underbrush. As the molecules of nature break down, their ashes become alive and rich with nutrients, ready to slip into the earth to feed and restore it to health.

Didn't I read somewhere that some trees, after surviving a fire, grow thicker bark to prepare for next time?

Why do meadows in the forest seem to appear out of nowhere? Were they burn areas at one time? Perhaps they are like silos, serving as a retreat for the seeds left behind after something burned the top. No one knows unless the meadow wishes to tell. Or, unless someone has a need or wants to learn why, and he bends down and feels the soil between his fingers. Eventually, a survival story will rise from that burned ground. The seeds will find their way down and plant deep. They will once again experience communion with the elements, finding their purpose. Then, they must discover the reason for the darkness, crack it open, and reach for the light.

An overgrown dense forest blocks the sunlight. Fungi grows in the thick, dank terrain. A fire starts and thins out the canopy. Sunlight now reaches the forest floor once again.

These are the images I had in my mind as I looked upon my irreparably damaged home. I focused on one thing in particular—the roof. It was collapsed in some places and vented in others. Sunlight poured through.

Could this be the Refiner's fire?

Left beside the burned craftsman, the raw form of metal rested in the crucible. The flames continued to heat to the maximum temperature. The smelter stood over the Refiner's fire; he poured off the dross and only purity, be it gold or silver, remained.

I stood under the pierced roof. Water dripped on my head. Sunlight warmed up my cheeks, providing a pathway for my own liquid regret to stream down my face.

In that moment, I knew what God wanted—an authentic relationship with me. With His resources and my humility, I trusted Him to carry me through. I relied on Him to know my own truth. On that very day, God filtered His nutrients into my soul. A rejuvenating strength was planted within me as the weeds of unworthiness were plucked away by His gracious hand, one painful yank at a time. God sheltered me just enough, but He also guided me to places where I needed to be exposed to His mercies. He always provided a tender covering. The bark of my soul started to regrow; this time, much thicker. The canopy over my heart was thinning out, allowing the warmth of His hope to filter through.

His presence became very evident in the regrowth of my life. His indelible grace became like invisible water buckets, a hydrant of a holy work in the inferno yet to come.

~~~

We staggered into the motel room. It was definitely not a vacation destination. Two double beds sat side by side, separated only by a nightstand with a lamp and a phone on it. The door faced out toward the main street of our town. It opened for us, but I didn't want it to close us in. Thick drapes darkened an already dark place. We stayed here for the next few weeks, courtesy of the Red Cross. Denny's served us meals that we paid for with vouchers.

Tim, in a good place with his health at the time, courted a new girlfriend. He hoped she might come to Thanksgiving dinner with us at my sister's house. A friend took in our dog and our cat remained at the vet until her lungs improved.

"What started the fire?"

So many people asked that dreaded question, but I didn't have an answer. I could only guess based off of what the firemen told me—a spark began around the washer and dryer. That morning, I had stuffed a heaping load of laundry into the washing machine. Both machines were cycling when I left for work. A howling wind, determined to break through, might've come up from under the garage door and wreaked its havoc.

I also knew that Corey indulged in smoking even though he knew I vehemently detested and discouraged it. Both he and I were questioned by an investigator; this became a heavy burden on both my heart and his. The local paper delivered our tragic story on the front page. One line in the article highlighted the possibility that the fire was started by a carelessly discarded cigarette by a teenager living in the house.

After a lot of hard work, I had hoped for that year to be Corey's year to shine. He had returned to his high school after spending a brief time at an alternative school. He had rejoined the football team and his graduation was just a few months away. Now I felt unbalanced and my hope for him teetered backward. I felt the need to grasp onto my kids with all I had.

My husband found solace in Christian alternative music. He tuned it in on the radio dial long before it became a go-to in my car. He traveled far for his job and needed to focus on good things during those long drives.

God orchestrated an amazing work in our lives. We started to see the goodness of community and belonging to a church body as we experienced the tangible blessings of prayer. God didn't cause death, sickness, accidents, poverty, abuse, or addiction; they were the results of a broken world that is in desperate need of Jesus. All of those things break the heart of God, more so than they break ours. I knew that I had broken God's heart by choosing to follow my own plan rather than His. Now, I needed to sit down and have a long dialogue with my Father. Romans 8:28 reverberated in my mind, "…God causes all things to work together for good…" The very verse I had hidden in my heart over many years now revealed God's hope for me in this hard season.

I prayed for forgiveness for having a doubtful, unrealized life. I asked God to show me how these ashes might bring our family to see Him more clearly. The sifting began, both literally and spiritually.

Restoration always takes time. With our own hands and the help of a few others, we tore out the burnt rubble, the roof, the garage, the drywall, and the carpet. I found grace in almost every moment of the process, a reassurance that God remained near to us. I was also well aware that some people were less than agreeable to our situation and timeline. I saw the destructive power of words, seeing how they can burn across a tender, vulnerable heart and scorch a relationship.

Despite some negative things, good people showed up…a lot of them. Thanks to the kindness of strangers, we rented a storage unit for the furniture we were able to salvage from the fire. Our house was stripped clean. The foundation lay bare, ash gathered in the corners, and a faint smell of what happened remained in the wind. God's Word gave me the key to drawing out a blueprint for living.

Corey soon migrated back to the neighborhoods and friends that supported his addictions. Meanwhile, Tim's short-lived girlfriend vanished with the winds of change and his anxiety ramped up. We moved in with my sister and her family and stayed until after Christmas.

Eventually, the blue buckets that held our essential belongings found their way back to Chino to a motel next to the freeway. Some nights I drove around searching for Corey. Other nights I lay awake in bed hoping he'd call me and ask to be picked up. Tim, now laden in maladies and symptoms, kept us busy with doctors and trips to the ER. He also concerned us with places he chose to unwind at, such as the local pool hall and karaoke bar. As for me, I was the description of a needy mess. Slowly, friends and family began to distance themselves. In that season, dependence on God alone became very clear.

We lived—*survived*—for three months in the motel. Some days I walked into the rental office to find our week's rent had been paid by "Anonymous." Ted worked his regular job and two extra jobs on the side to support our family. Eventually, we gathered at the house to clean and repair it, deciding we would rebuild it ourselves.

My cat, Puff, did not improve and I had to make the hard decision to put her down. Our dog, Chance, was very needy himself and he soon out energized the friends who decided to take him in. Grateful that they watched over him for a time, we brought Chance back to the house. He stood guard every day, waiting for our morning and afternoon visits. Though the fire happened in November, we did not receive our first check from the insurance company until February.

Perspective, as well as insight, dwindled a bit of its light, focusing on the dark landscape of the aftermath. I needed to admit and learn from my mistakes. I wanted to find hope through the tragedy. I sought to see the good in people and I believed in recovery.

Over the next four years, I withdrew into myself, living in places I started calling "caves." I poured myself into trusting God with everything. I wanted His will, not my own. Life did not get easier. Tim's physical and emotional health—chronic at times, critical at others—demanded all of our energy. Corey began to separate himself from toxic influences, but his trust issues remained. Deep within my spirit, I knew the slow progress of the house and our financial situation seemed impossible. I wanted to believe with all my heart that God intended for us to return to the Verdugo Avenue house. However, every day, something wanted to remind me of my failures.

When the fire report came back about six months after the fire, the cause listed by the investigator was "Unknown." When I read those words, I knew God had rescued my son from the stigma of doubt, stamping out that last ember of possible guilt he held onto. I let it go as well. It didn't matter to me anymore. We needed to move forward.

~~~

Motel life—footsteps outside your door, strangers, a broken car window, theft in the middle of the night, ants, food poisoning, anger, loss of privacy, laundromats, 911 calls, loneliness, embarrassment, cockroaches, drunk and abusive neighbors, humble reflection, God's provision, music, grace, hope...

It was a mixed up and dizzy life, and I prayed for grace to steady me as I sunk my feet into the foundation of my faith. I prayed for revelation to become the roof over my head, and for forgiveness and love to become the two-by-fours on which to frame a better life. As I opened up and discovered the truth of where God wanted me to be in all this, I discovered strength in Him. He loved me and had a purpose for me, even in the hardest challenges of my life.

He rid me of the underbrush of a fruitless life. I began to see, in the depths of grasping onto my family so tight, how God held me, instructed me, and allowed His sunlight to filter and grow me. I cried a lot. Tears helped me to filter out what could be kept, what needed to be discarded, what could be restored, and what needed a new place to call home. Teardrops of nutrients surrendered to the forest floor of my scorched soul.

One day, Ted walked in the door of the little apartment we rented. In his authority from God, as the head of our home, he said, "Coke," (as I am affectionately called by many), "We can't do this anymore."

I knew what he meant, but I did not want to hear. It was a clear choice between saving our family or the house.

His boss purchased the property out from under us; it was about a third of the way complete at the time. The company Ted worked for finished the rebuild and flipped it. I never went back inside, walked through the halls, or stood at the newly hung front door. Though abounding grace once lived there, the same grace upon grace went with me wherever I found my family. I became more attuned to His presence and I started to seek Him in my own personal restoration.

God's Word seemed to confirm all that I began to process.

"For He stands at the right hand of the needy,
to save him from those who judge his soul."
— Psalm 109:31

Another door began to open, but the entrance seemed foreboding. I stood on that threshold for many more months, pulling Tim back from the edge. Pain pounded against the door. Painkillers answered. The door slammed shut, but I pried it open again and again, leading my son out with all the love a mother holds for her firstborn child. He straddled the entryway. I couldn't imagine what was waiting on the other side, for Tim and for me.

I knew that desperate people often make the wrong choices, especially when pain burns deep in their lungs.

Chapter 6

Grace Gifts

"You therefore, my son,
be strong in the grace that is in Christ Jesus."
— 2 Timothy 2:1

What is grace? Is it getting away with something, or being pardoned for something? Is it a noun or a verb? Is it just a recited prayer at mealtimes? Is it something supernatural or miraculous? What is the difference between regular grace and amazing grace? Is there one? Do you recognize living in grace every day, as a resource for strength and for the will to carry on?

My hope for you, friend, is that you and grace will meet each other in whatever circumstances you find yourself.

My continued prayer is that you will dive deep into that grace and see its intricate details and facets, like a shimmering diamond.

My joy for you, beloved of God, is when amazing grace becomes recognized and planted so deep within your heart that its roots fill up the emptiness and surge through the loneliness.

My desire for you is that you continue to apply that grace in the pruning way of regrets and doubts, and that you bloom in your season to carry on in God's purpose.

My call to you is to discover and use those grace gifts that God gives to all of His children and share them with others around you.

My vision for you is that you will see with an eternal perspective and, in the strength of that grace, know that God is good!

~~~

When I was nine years old, I had a Vacation Bible School teacher named Grace Cubak. When she talked about Jesus, the room lit up.

"God loved the whole world so much that He died for me and you!" She would passionately explain. She'd grab our hands and hold them as she prayed that we would love Jesus too. She told us the story of how He died on a cross so that we could live forever. She told us that all we had to do was ask Him for help, pray, and believe.

I thought about what Grace Cubak told me a lot. One night, I climbed into my bed, closed my eyes, and prayed to God in heaven. I wanted to love God like Grace did. I knew I needed God in my heart. I didn't understand the Spirit and all that Christianity encompassed, but I knew I wanted to be a part of it.

I probably prayed something like this, "Dear Jesus, I believe in You and I know I have sinned. Please forgive me and be my Savior. Help me to be good and go to heaven someday. Amen."

Grace, the person, led me to grace, the Savior. Grace upon grace, truth upon truth, sovereignty, and purpose—I grew in the understanding of this amazing love. God reconnected my broken soul back to His divine purpose and granted it a lifetime-plus-eternity guarantee with a no-return policy.

As the Jenga tower of my life came crashing down after the fire, God clearly began to hand me the pieces again, one by one. He showed me how to place them and how to process the loss. This grace gave me an insight into God's forgiveness more than I had known before. A new intimacy with God's Spirit began to transform me into someone more authentic and transparent.

I'd like to ask whoever is reading this book to think about your own relationship with God—His gift of grace to you. Have you fully received all God has prepared for you? Do you recognize it when you are in need? Do you see it when life is good? Do you seek it when life is not so good?

The Apostle Paul wrote, "In Him we have redemption through His blood, the forgiveness of our trespasses, according to the riches of His grace which He lavished on us" (Ephesians 1:7-8).

Can you picture grace, like riches, piled upon you? How does someone live in and through that perspective when their life has been permanently shadowed by a tragedy?

My hope for this story is that God's goodness, divine purpose, and will, coupled with the reader's intentional seeking of Him, will guide him or her to understand moments from an eternal perspective and to move forward in His love and light.

~~~

During this season of my life, I grew. I experienced moments in the dry, wind-whipped desert. I was in desperate need of a transplant and pruning. The path I started traveling down was one of numerous detours and side streets. My human nature and influences started leading me astray, out of God's will and into my own. Even in those days, God's grace never left me.

It was like a dimmer switch had been put in my soul… How could I see what was hiding in the shadows? God waited and stirred within me, encouraging me to walk by faith. In my seeking to understand more of this grace, strength and trust developed a more mature faith within my soul. A story began to unfold out of the ashes; the Lord wove a beautiful tapestry from threads that seemed weak and stretched.

After a grim season, I began the slow and steady process of returning to His grace and soaking in all of His promises. There was so much awaiting me, deeper in God's grace; He was calling me to seek Him wholeheartedly. To ignore that call would be like opening one present on Christmas Eve and forgetting about the rest on Christmas morning… Seeing a beautiful sunrise, but ignoring a beautiful sunset later that evening… Wiggling your toes in the sand and strolling into the refreshing surf, but stepping over the beautiful seashell where a pearl waits inside…

No one truly knew the journey we were on with our chronically ill son, nor did they understand the decisions we were forced to make in order to survive our difficult circumstances. I pulled inward, into God in a way that I had never pushed myself before. I infused Him more and more into my daily routine. It was like seeing with a brand-new set of eyes, a fresh insight opening up within me. A generous amount of grace deposited itself into my heart. The connections to God became brighter. I had received grace after praying for salvation as a child, but I needed so much more love and life to stir up my soul and bring me closer to God. I was more motivated than ever to seek the grace gifts He had for me.

I needed His grace more than I knew.

In the depths of despair, I recognized His grace more. I recognized His heavenly touches as He intentionally and personally met me in the dark corners of my soul to flood me with hope. I possessed a new longing for Him which I tapped into daily for continued strength. I experienced His constant, never-ending goodness in and through the coming months.

I clung wholeheartedly to the grace which continued to surround me in love.

Grace and the amazing God who generously delivered it displayed His unconditional love for me, which He also demonstrated on a cross set upon a lonely hill. He covered the whole world with this grace, manifesting it tangibly on the day He was crucified. I committed myself to living in and by this grace once again.

God also showed Himself in my journaling, in my connections with the people around me, in my quiet moments and daily devotions, in the gifts He slowly started to reveal in me, and in the beauty of nature that only a divine artist and sculptor could have imagined. Joyful music sung a new harmony in my heart.

"For of His fullness we have all received,
and grace upon grace."
— John 1:16

His saving grace gave me a promise. His sustaining grace allowed me to climb out of my grief and seek His will in and through the gifts He continued to give me. His amazing grace filled me with hope. His everlasting grace flew ahead of me and prepared a way for something I would have never expected.

~~~

Through journaling and writing, I began to see God in a bigger way. So many grace gifts sat unopened for so many years. My heart longed for peace and my soul begged for an opportunity to reopen a dialogue with the Lord. The notebook which was later transformed into a journal became my "Facetime" with the Lord. He pulled me into a deeper relationship with Himself, preparing my heart for what was to come.

~~~

One stressful afternoon, I sat down with my journal and

Bible. I opened up to Ephesians 6 and began reading. The words of the Apostle Paul explained that a Christian life is sometimes like being in a war. Like a soldier, I needed to prepare for battle.

Words in my head began to rhyme. Sometimes the words I wrote down were like a narrative, but other times they were lyrical and poetic. I liked both and God used both to minister to me. I scribbled these pain-filled thoughts into my journal...

Will it be a night spent waiting in the emergency room?
Or will it be a night of anxiety and pain at home?

Tim, now 26 years old, was still battling with chronic kidney disease. He had also developed pulmonary hypertension as a result of massive blood clots in his system.

I was exhausted and completely overwhelmed with constant worrying, trips to the doctor's office, and my son's dependency on pain medicine. Every day presented a new challenge. Tim's life hung in the balance.

Deep within me, my soul cried out.

Lord, I need a moment.

I collapsed at the kitchen table, desperately needing time to pray. I conversed with God in my writing. Next to me, there was a stack of tattered and stained journals filled with my anxieties, prayers, and praises. I penned the date at the top of a new page—February 7, 2007. I needed strength and courage to survive the unexpected battle that was coming my way.

I finished reading Ephesians 6 and turned back to my journal. I scribbled down a rhyming prayer. Though I was weary from battle already, I felt more equipped to combat my discouragement. I began writing, praying for grace and relief. I pictured myself as a solider and our family as a regiment standing on the front lines.

"Put on the full armor of God, so that you will be able to stand firm against the schemes of the devil.

For our struggle is not against flesh and blood, but against the rulers, against the powers, against the world forces of this darkness, against the spiritual forces of wickedness in the heavenly places.

Therefore, take up the full armor of God, so that you will be able to resist in the evil day, and having done everything, to stand firm.

Stand firm therefore, having girded your loins with truth, and having put on the breastplate of righteousness, and having shod your feet with the preparation of the gospel of peace; in addition to all, taking up the shield of faith with which you will be able to extinguish all the flaming arrows of the evil one.

And take the helmet of salvation, and the sword of the Spirit, which is the word of God.

With all prayer and petition pray at all times in the Spirit, and with this in view, be on the alert with all perseverance and petition for all the saints..."

— Ephesians 6:11-18

Before the end of the month, the words from my poem "To Give You the Glory" would be put to the test.

~~~

To Give You the Glory

Inspired by Ephesians 6:11-18
A prayer for strength and courage

Swirling around like a drain full of muck,
My head is busy with bothersome junk.
Clogged and stopped up, no progress made,
The worries and doubts I wish to fade.

I'm not focused, should read Your Word,
The devil wants a holy purge.
I know You, can feel You, waiting in the wings;
Clear my mind of disruptive things.

This is for sure, the devil's cruel tool...
Feed on my weakness and make me a fool.
But I am aware of his tricky scheme.
Fight it with an armor, shiny, it gleams.

Days are rough and storms lie ahead,
Usually bad planning or not being fed
By Your Word, or asking for wisdom, you see.
But sometimes, it's just God's lessons for me.

Faith and trust, done this before.
A lifestyle it should be, it's You I need more.
Disciplined life so evil won't prevail.
Help me now Jesus, with You I won't fail.

Slip into the armor, Your Word covers all.
With prayer joints move; on You I do call.
Knowledge and wisdom, on firm ground I stand.
I'm never alone, held by Your hand.

Your Truth surrounds me, assurance it gives.
March with righteousness, a pure heart that lives.
Prepare for battle with worldly thoughts,
The devil, he deals in unrighteous plots.

By faith, I shield the fiery darts,
That seek to destroy the forgiven hearts.
Salvation: the helmet I proudly wear,
The Holy Spirit: my sword, I go forth, prepared.

I'm stronger now Lord, after saying this prayer,
And reading Your Word in Ephesians is where
Strength and courage for the battle I find,
I give You the Glory, Lord. Nothing is mine.

PLAYLIST II

Breathe

1. "Harder to Breathe" — Maroon 5
2. "Night Drive" — The All-American Rejects
3. "In My Room" — The Beach Boys
4. "You Were There" — Eric Clapton
5. "Somewhere in the Middle" — Casting Crowns
6. "Trying" — Lifehouse
7. "In My Life" — The Beatles
8. "My Last Breath" — Evanescence
9. "Dead Wrong" — The Fray
10. "Springs of Life" — Ginny Owens
11. "Free" — Ginny Owens
12. "If I Should Fall Behind" — Faith Hill
13. "What This World Needs" — Casting Crowns
14. "I Know You're There" — Casting Crowns

Chapter 7

At the River's Side

We entered the doors of yet another emergency room, searching for a miracle doctor for Timmy. He loved his kidney doctor, Dr. Khan, but his lungs and heart were proving to be more of an issue now.

Are not our hearts always the issue?

A question kept repeating in my mind... What are we willing to believe and put our faith in when just breathing becomes a burden?

In the next city, just 30 minutes down the freeway, Tim found himself in the wrong hospital with the wrong insurance yet again.

"This kid's got serious medical issues," every doctor Tim met said. Even though he was 26 years old, he didn't look a day over 18.

Over the last four years, we encountered so many tough times. We lost our home to an unexplainable fire, and we lived in several different places ranging from musty motels to small apartments. We finally got settled into an actual rental house. I worked just around the corner and Tim had a bedroom to himself again. I thought the new arrangement would help his anxiety and get his sleeping pattern back to normal.

Unfortunately, I no longer knew what normal looked or felt like. Nobody in our family did. For the last few years, our normal was driving to emergency rooms at one in the morning, stacking our cabinets full of medicine bottles, and praying we'd survive as a family.

Christ came to pull us out of our normal and bring us into the supernatural.

"He's a very sick young man. We have yet to identify the type of pneumonia settled into his compromised lungs," the doctor reported to us.

In the ICU, Tim bonded immediately with a nurse named D'Anna. She fell victim to his charm and she also loved the Lord.

God is good as He orchestrates His grace.

In the days to come, recalling our new normal, that laughing moment I shared with my son would come to mean everything I placed my hope in.

~~~

We gathered in the living room. I had just come in from work and slung my book bag onto the floor next to the couch. I sat down next to Tim, who flipped furiously through the channels to find whatever sports game he could. It was silent for a moment. Then, suddenly, a loud noise came from…where? My bag?

The sound had startled both of us; then we busted into laughter as I pulled my battery-operated pencil sharpener from the bag.

It was a small, silly moment, but I saw God's goodness and sovereignty through it. With Him, every moment was an opportunity to receive grace. Grace, when given, sharpened and humbled. God's plan was to use us to sharpen others for His greater glory.

"And He has said to me, 'My grace is sufficient for you, for power is perfected in weakness.'"
— 2 Corinthians 12:9

~~~

Three days… Four days… Still no improvement…

Tim's oxygen levels were very low. A nurse mentioned intubation, another talked about a breathing machine. The date was Thursday, February 22, 2007.

Like every time before, I suspected he'd show signs of improvement. He had survived so much already, so I counted on him coming home and staying there longer this time. We made arrangements to meet with a new primary care doctor in Orange County on March 1.

He wanted to come home. He always did.

"The Spirit of God has made me, and the breath of the Almighty gives me life."
— Job 33:4

~~~

The group of elders I called from my home church prepared themselves to drive out to Riverside, a city situated on the Santa Ana River.

"He who believes in Me, as the Scripture said, 'From his innermost being will flow rivers of living water.'"
— John 7:38

From Tim's innermost being—his personality, his spirit, his precocious tenacity to be the center of attention—flowed a lot of life.

Sometimes, while in the hospital, he'd call me really late at night. "Mom, can you bring me some French fries? I need some Skittles…"

Because I was his mother, I had 24-hour access to his room. Most of the time, I'd cater to his requests. I would sit up with him and watch the news and usually the first part of *The Tonight Show.* We would laugh for a while until a nurse came in with medicine for him to take. When she'd encourage me to go home, I'd kiss Tim's forehead and say goodnight.

Now he lay in Riverside… At the River's side…

I arrived at the hospital later than normal on Friday night. It was cold and rainy. The elders had paid their visit and Tim told me all about their prayers and conversations. I was sorry I'd missed them.

While at the hospital that night, I heard about a young woman and her baby who were driving and flew off the freeway. The mom didn't make it, but miraculously, her baby survived without a scratch. I found out later that the mom was the daughter of a former customer of mine from my previous job. Young and beautiful, she was close in age to Tim. Her car had landed near the same river over 30 miles away.

At the River's side...

Tim received his dinner and I fed him with a spoon, just small bites at a time. I watched him swallow and accept the sustenance of life. An endless stream of tubes, monitors, and IVs floated around a mother and her son in a hospital room in Riverside. We became well-acquainted with that shoreline. Grace soon began to gather along the banks, pooling around bushes and spilling over boulders.

At the River's side...

> *"He sends forth springs in the valleys;*
> *they flow between the mountains..."*
> *— Psalm 104:10*

Chapter 8

What I Know

Turkey and a little bit of mashed potatoes… I continued to encourage him to eat, but he just wanted to talk.

"Mom, I hear music," he said.

"The TV isn't on, Tim."

"I still hear music. It's your pencil sharpener."

"My pencil sharpener? I don't have my book bag here."

"Yeah, Mom. I hear it. It's singing."

"The pencil sharpener is singing?" *The pain meds must be working…* "What's it singing?"

And he sang.

I knew the song.

Later that night, we hugged. I tucked him in and kissed his head. After, I walked past the curtain that separated his room from the central nurse station. I said goodbye to D'Anna and the others.

Saying goodbye…

I drove home in the mist of the night. Praise music ministered to my heart from the radio. When I got home, I crawled into bed and relayed to Ted my hope for our son's recovery after seeing a glimpse of his spunky personality.

Ted and I awoke Saturday, February 24 to car problems and our own health concerns. We both had bronchitis; we were hacking and infected. I can't remember what the exact car issues were now, but I do remember how rotten we both felt that day. We talked with Tim several times over the phone in between our coughing attacks. His pneumonia was improving, but his kidneys were still having issues. They always were.

At 3:00 AM on Sunday, the phone rang.

"We had to intubate your son," the nurse relayed. "Get here in the morning as soon as you can."

His oxygen levels had dropped to less than 40% that night. The nurse reassured me that intubation would help him get the oxygen he needed to recover. He would be weaned off of it as he got stronger, but for now he was in an induced coma.

"Cease striving and know…"
— Psalm 46:10

Our prayers immediately went up. The word quickly got out about Tim's worsening condition and, one by one, prayer warriors and friends gathered with us. They filled an entire room.

My son was still, a noisy machine breathing and monitoring for him. I watched his numbers with anticipation and expectation.

Out of the pumping life-machine came a rhythm. It wasn't a stanza or a chorus, but a plucking of a certain chord, like the tapping of fingers against a steering wheel or the swaying of a head to a beating heart.

I don't know the words to this song. I'll stay up all night to hear it though.

We camped out at the hospital—slumped, gathered, coughed, stared. We did our own breathing treatments in a tent of tender mercies alongside our friends.

The next Sunday, my pastor resigned. No one wanted to tell me.

I pray what I know.

I pray what I know about the character of God to be true.

I pray about how to prepare for what I do not know.

WHATEVER IS TRUE

Our Father who is in heaven,

WHATEVER IS HONORABLE

hallowed be Your name.

WHATEVER IS RIGHT

Your kingdom come. Your will be done,

on earth as it is in heaven.

WHATEVER IS PURE

Give us this day our daily bread.

WHATEVER IS LOVELY

And forgive us our debts, as we also have forgiven our debtors.

WHATEVER IS OF GOOD REPUTE

And do not lead us into temptation,

IF THERE IS ANY EXCELLENCE

but deliver us from evil.

AND IF ANYTHING WORTHY OF PRAISE

DWELL ON THESE THINGS

For Yours is the kingdom and the power

and the glory forever. Amen.

— Philippians 4:8; Matthew 6:9-13

Chapter 9

On This Day

On Monday, February 26 things changed again. Blood started to show through the clear line that went into Tim's nostrils. We split the time up with 15-minute shifts where each person had a chance to go into his room, talk to him, and encourage him to keep fighting. Most of Timmy's best friends stood nearby. Some of our close friends and family waited, watched, and prayed with us.

His kidney output started slowing down and the blood in the tubes no longer seemed like a "no big deal" sort of event. I quieted down, sinking deeper into my introverted self. My spirit was bleeding internally, hemorrhaging at my son's condition and all of the "what ifs." Yet, I held onto hope. I curled up and prayed.

At some horrible, silent hour on Monday morning, a scope and camera procedure gave the medical professionals evidence they did not wish to relay to us. They could not curtail Tim's blood loss without surgery. However, surgery, they said, was way too risky. The news drained our resolve. Many people gathered around us, taking care of us in these dark hours.

On Tuesday, February 27, a nurse approached us. She told us that a "brilliant surgeon" wanted to do the surgery to find the bleeding source in Tim's gut and stop it.

When we met the surgeon, he explained, "He will probably lose half of his stomach, but it's a chance to take."

Half his stomach? I couldn't even fathom his words. *He's already lost half his lungs and his kidneys don't work right either! And now you want to damage his stomach? He's going to be so mad at me...*

A lonely sense of grief began to settle in my heart, as well as a slight bit of guilt over the fact that I didn't want this hotshot doctor attempting surgery on my son. It was more cutting and more dissecting, but it could be Tim's hope. I knew my son—how tired he was, how much pain he lived in on a daily basis, and how compromised his active life had become. I wanted him to be free and healed.

Encouragement refilled my husband and our weary support system. I wasn't sure what I felt, but I knew the presence of the Lord was with us. On that day, God continued to ask me to trust Him. He reassured me that He would continue to give me strength.

My husband looked me in the eyes and said, "We have to try."

He cried. I bent down to kiss him and then we prayed together. We stood and watched Tim's gurney get pushed through the double doors.

Later that afternoon, I walked to the hospital chapel. I sat, waited, cried, and prayed in silence. Ted was with me for a little while, but eventually he grew restless and left to be closer to the doors that yielded to hope. Inside the chapel, I was beyond numb. I pictured Tim's blood, the blood of Jesus, and the conversation I would have with my son when he woke up. I prayed for his stomach to be whole. I prayed for a miracle. I closed my eyes and sought my Creator's face.

I know You are a good God. I know I am loved. I know You love Timmy. Be with us, Lord...

Timothy met the Lord that day. God granted a miraculous healing—one that only comes by being drawn into the arms of the Father. On that day, I let my son go and be with his Creator. On that day, an eternal perspective became my reality. On that day, my life changed. On that day, Jesus as my Lord and Savior was not just what I believed, but it was what I breathed, both in my inhale and exhale.

I walked out of the chapel and saw Ted and my lifelong friend, Lynn, walking toward me. Ted was shaking his head and crying. The look on his face alone told me that Tim did not survive the surgery. He took his last breath only 20 minutes into the operation.

On that day, February 27, 2007, somewhere around 5:45 PM, grace and mercy tied their canoe to the River's side. Tim had been living in a dry and weary land for too long, and his healing came when he passed from his earthly life. He entered the boat of eternity, receiving God's answer to our desperate prayers.

On that day, he was healed.

On that day, he stepped into eternity.

On that day, I began to seek God's purpose, comfort, and understanding. Within each one of those, I received a generous portion along that same River's edge, where gentle, lapping waves of grace upon grace resided.

Chapter 10

Because of the Blood

Timmy's favorite nurse, D'Anna, started her shift at 7:00 PM. Concerned colleagues intercepted her before she got to her floor at the ICU. More of our family friends started to show up. At one point, I remember collapsing to the floor. In that moment, I realized that grief was not only an emotional pain, but a physical one too. Everything ached deeply.

My sweet pastor arrived at the hospital not long after. He may have left the pulpit at our church, but not the service of his congregates. In need of grace himself, he served us with deep compassion and comfort.

A lot more went on behind the scenes; flat tires were fixed, phone calls were made, and provisions were given to us. God showed His grace to us through His people.

"But when the kindness of God our Savior and His love for mankind appeared, He saved us, not on the basis of deeds which we have done in righteousness, but according to His mercy, by the washing of regeneration and renewing by the Holy Spirit, whom He poured out upon us richly through Jesus Christ our Savior, so that being justified by His grace we would be made heirs according to the hope of eternal

D'Anna probably broke a rule by getting too emotionally involved with a patient, but in her own distress, she came alongside us and asked our permission to serve Tim one final time.

With dutiful courage, she asked, "May I serve you and Timmy by washing him before you see him?"

We obliged without hesitation. She wasn't a stranger, and she had doted on and cared for Tim for those six days he was in the hospital. She bonded with us in our shared belief in Jesus Christ and in the instant affection she allowed herself to have for our son. All in a matter of six days...

"As each one has received a special gift, employ it in serving one another as good stewards of the manifold grace of God."
— 1 Peter 4:10

God anoints and washes those who come to Him. It is by His Son's blood that we are made clean. Jesus' sacrifice erased our sins, imperfections, and scars. His blood anointed us. His blood washed us.

Sometimes kidneys don't filter and blood clots form, clogging up the lungs. Sometimes men go off to war and meet IEDs, returning home in flag-draped coffins. Sometimes 17-year-olds get bone cancer and college-bound freshmen hit their heads on a rock while diving into a lake. Sometimes teens drive off the side of a mountain or burn to death in an off-roading accident. Sometimes a broken heart shuts off in the middle of the night. Sometimes an eight-year-old rides his bike into the middle of the street. Sometimes babies go down for a nap and don't wake up. Sometimes football players collapse on the field during practice and never stand again.

Youth is not a guarantee for life, but Jesus is.

Mercy lathered up a washcloth and love administered the final massage while an eagle took flight. He soared with mighty strength and a wise eye, taking in all of creation. He swooped down with lightning speed and rose up again with grace and fortitude. He glided with the winds and flew above the highest peaks. He climbed the cliffs and skimmed the great seas. He knew he was loved. He returned where that love completed him. He went home.

We spent several hours with Tim. Pastor Dane worked his words to stall the mortician so that some of Tim's friends could see him before he was taken away. He was finally free of tubes, machines, and pain.

Your weary days are behind you, son. Your tired and relentless pursuits are vanquished.

~~~

I wrote a poem four months before Tim passed. It was a slightly frustrating day, as our car problems added up to a boiling point. As I journaled that night, this poem captured my thoughts. I wrote it in Tim's voice, with his angst and passion. The scene that I described unfolded on our drive home from the hospital.

I tried to capture some of Tim's personality in it—his anxiety and his spiritual questioning. Perfection comes to no one and chronic pain only ramps up a person's irritability factor; yet, in the bad days and the good days, the Lord is loving. Whether we are rotten or righteous, questioning or faithful, the Holy Spirit ministers to us, Jesus Christ loves us, and God reigns eternal.

"The Lord is good, a stronghold in the day of trouble,
and He knows those who take refuge in Him."
— Nahum 1:7

~~~

Dry

The car overheated!
Not what we needed!
I don't feel good, God, as You know.
Is this old car ready to blow?

Relief please, from this position
Sitting here, with distortion.
Bloated with water and such
My kidneys not relieving me much.

Just get to the pizza place
Don't stall out!
Agitated, anxious,
"I hate this car," I shout.

Mom grabs the pizza I want to taste
Food and drink calm my pace.
But the dashboard shows "H" I see,
Steam and smoke in front of me.

Limping along about two blocks
This car makes funny sounding knocks.
"God, are you listening? Please make the light green."
Why such a stressful scene?

Finally, my neighborhood is close to us.
I think we'll make it despite all the fuss.
Cool down the car and me as well.
Home is where I want to dwell.

The car just needed water,
Dried to the bone, the cause of the matter.
Not me though, I have fluid to spare!
Sometimes I wonder, does God really care?

Car runs fine now, radiator too dry
Refilled with water for the next drive-by.
Can there be something to give to me?
"Refresh me, rejuvenate me!" I plea.

Filled up with fluid, a swollen bod.
You ask about my spirit, my space for God?
Am I dried up? Can the Lord refill me?
Okay, be still and think a bit.

I remember the story, about Living Water
From God's Word, Jesus is the teacher.
If I drink of this Water, I will never thirst.

Lord, sometimes I feel I am just cursed.

I believe you, Lord, but my faith is weak
Help me to pray, be the One I seek.
A broken soul; I need a helping hand.
Thank you for loving me. I wish I knew the plan.

~~~

"O God, You are my God; I shall seek You earnestly;
my soul thirsts for You, my flesh yearns for You,
in a dry and weary land where there is no water."
— *Psalm 63:1*

Timothy, our son, was now quenched and immersed in eternity. As for me, I waded in a pool of grief and sadness. Beginner swimming lessons stood ahead, which included learning to float, dog paddling, knowing when to hang on and when to let go, and how to control my breathing.

Lord, help me to just come up for air.

Chapter 11

Mourning in a New Morning

"Surely my soul remembers and is bowed down within me.
This I recall to my mind, therefore I have hope.
The Lord's lovingkindnesses indeed never cease,
for His compassions never fail.
They are new every morning; great is Your faithfulness."
— Lamentations 3:20-23

We arrived home late. The heavy waves hit us again as we entered through the doorway. Drained, sick, and inconsolable, the water washed us ashore and left us gasping for air. I felt alone and I longed to feel him, yet I knew that Tim had reached a distant, peaceful shore. During this time, home was where all of the relentless, grief-filled thoughts came crashing in. The reality of my son's absence hit me hard.

I needed something tangible to hold on to, and I knew exactly what it would be. I floundered through his drawers until I found it—his favorite blue and yellow striped golf shirt. I held it close. I slept with it under my cheeks for many weeks; it absorbed my tears and prayers, acting as a buoy through the many long nights.

Morning finally came, but I had only slept two or three hours at best. I remember rising, but I felt like a zombie, crippled by my grief. I walked into the kitchen to get some coffee. I cried nearly as much as I breathed.

I sipped at my coffee. I was thinking, but I didn't want to. I was breathing, but I felt as though I didn't know how. I wanted out of my own body and mind.

Then I heard it...

Music... A song... A conversation...

Tim's voice came flooding back into my mind. It was the song he had sang to me, the song he knew, the song of all songs. Timmy was singing it and the Lord's presence was filling me with an overwhelming, riveting, saturating peace. My hands shook and my chest heaved with sobs, but the Holy Spirit poured His grace into the broken pieces of my heart and filtered His love through my veins.

I heard the whole conversation again, ringing in my ears.

"Mom, I hear music... Your pencil sharpener is singing to me."

"What's it singing, Tim?"

Amazing grace, how sweet the sound
That saved a wretch like me
I once was lost, but now I'm found
Was blind, but now I see

I didn't understand how I could be so crushed with grief yet so rejuvenated by God's amazing grace. A supernatural dichotomy blossomed in my mind as righteous prayers wasted no time in providing the sweet oxygen I needed to stay afloat.

~~~

Busyness ministered within the walls of our house. Friends started arriving and doing—oh, so much doing! Food started to show up later that day—oh, so much food!

Eventually, Ted and I started to talk about the memorial service.

"There's something I need to tell you, Ted," I began. "I'm going to have to speak at Tim's service and give his eulogy. There's something that happened between us and I am the only one who can tell the story. God just brought it to my memory this morning. He wants me to share it."

"How can you do that?"

"I don't know. How am I going to do any of this? Do you want to know what happened?"

"No," Ted said. "I'll hear it at the same time everyone else does."

The next several days were spent making arrangements, taking phone calls, and planning a service. Ted and I carefully picked the music. No one in our family was musical, but we loved songs, beats, and lyrics that moved us to dance, cry, love, and celebrate. That's exactly what we wanted Tim's service to be—a celebration of his life.

We met with Jason, Tim's high school pastor, who was

now serving as our church's associate pastor. The date for the service was set for Thursday, March 8, and we requested that Jason officiate it. Everyone I asked to participate in the service graciously obliged and blessed us. Tim's junior high school pastor, Brett Kunkle, also spoke. A beautiful video was made under the amazing leadership of one of my closest friends, Cindy, and the technical skills of a few others from church. Food for after the celebration was organized, and checks came in the mail to help with the expenses. Two obituaries were written and submitted.

Somehow it all got done, which was a miracle in and of itself. It was the epitome of love in action. Meanwhile, I remained within the walls of this dichotomy of grief and love. Each one took up a residence in my heart.

Timmy passed away on a Tuesday. His service was planned and marked on the calendar for the following week on Thursday. The weekend slowly approached—a weekend Timmy had been looking forward to. He was supposed to attend the wedding of his very first and closest friend, Jody, and his fiancée, Susie. Though Jody was a few years older than Tim, they hung out a lot and loved each other deeply. I remember in 2001 when Tim had a 9-hour lung embolectomy; Jody had rallied a crowd of Tim's friends in support.

Though Tim wouldn't be in attendance, Ted and I knew we had to go to the wedding. The ceremony was going to take place at the Los Serranos Country Club—a place Tim frequented.

We arrived early and the ceremony started late, allowing

me time to slip into the bride's room and share a tear with Susie and Jody's sister, Jenny. They were both honored and surprised that we came. I explained to them that we wanted to partake in their happiness and represent Tim and all the memories we shared as families growing up on the same street.

The wedding was set up outside in a small garden. The white chairs and altar faced the trees, which were nearly bare from the winter. The air stood cool and still. We sat about four rows back next to the aisle. When the bridesmaids began their descent, a soft breeze started to blow.

Most people call them "dust devils," those mini whirlwinds that pick up leaves and paper, whirl them around at ground level, and seemingly come out of nowhere. As Jody and Susie recited their vows to one another, a dust devil appeared. It moved first to the left and then to the right at the bottom of the altar. It whipped up and around the top of the arch, then made its way back down the aisle, leaves twirling and dancing in its wake.

Everyone noticed.

Ted turned to me first. With glistening eyes, he said, "Timmy…"

I felt the same spiritual awareness.

"Let me introduce you to Mr. and Mrs. Jody Moreland!"

The happy couple kissed and turned to face the crowd. Jody walked past his parents, past Susie's family, and embraced us both.

"Did you see the wind?" he asked.

"Timmy's here," I told him.

Somehow, I knew this sort of thing might happen.

~~~

It was the night before Tim's service. I sat weeping at my keyboard, praying for the ability to talk about my son's life, the hours before his death, and the gift of the Lord. I wanted to talk about the song "Amazing Grace," the song that Tim and I shared. It was all surreal to me. At 1:00 AM, I opened God's Word and turned to the first book of the New Testament.

Lord, please make sense of my thoughts. Let this be what needs to be shared.

I felt as though at any moment I might turn into a roly-poly, closing in on myself and hiding. As soon as I opened the Microsoft Word document, memories, anecdotes, and love began to crawl across the page. I wanted to be honest, brave, and full of grace.

Grace, that amazing gift of a song that gave me peace the morning after, for I knew it ushered Timmy into heaven. Grace answered our prayers. Grace healed. The song Timmy sang assured me he knew of God's amazing grace. I set the Word of God in my lap and felt the Spirit of the Lord surround me, filling me with His strength.

"...do not worry about how or what you are to say; for it will be given you in that hour what you are to say."
— *Matthew 10:19*

"What I tell you in the darkness, speak in the light; and what you hear whispered in your ear, proclaim upon the housetops."
— *Matthew 10:27*

In that moment, these verses gave me the strength to write, and I would come to understand more of God and His purposes than ever before. A new morning dawned in my heart. God's light brought me insight and clarity to see beyond myself. I found myself wanting more of God because I knew only His intervention would give me the peace I needed. I knew my timeline with Timmy didn't end as long as God existed along every stretch of that line. The more I saw God in all of this, the more of His grace I received.

Grief is not a place you visit purposefully, but if someone is living in a season of grief, God's grace must be their navigator. This is what I knew—that many people were praying for us. This is what I didn't know—that I'd feel a whisper of God's love in the most unsuspecting moments, that I'd experience revelations and holy moments which would carry me through the months to come.

I'd soon be plunged into a continuum of grace upon amazing grace.

~~~

Tim's Eulogy

Our son, Timothy, was born on a warm Santa Ana day—September 25, 1980. He was our firstborn child, and the firstborn grandchild in our family. He was full of personality from the very beginning and he was a very good baby.

It was not long into Timmy's life that he realized when he fell asleep, the world was still doing things and he was missing out on it. He had an insatiable need to be informed. Timmy's joy was making sure you knew too! Information about his world was never something he kept to himself; he would quickly process and then "spread the word." No matter how trivial an event seemed to someone, it was of significance to Timmy. No one had a choice but to share in his enthusiasm.

He also loved to talk. One example of this was when Ted and I went to Vancouver for a week. Timmy was probably in the first grade or so. The first thing he informed us of when we picked him up from Grandma Joyce's house was what happened at Tiananmen Square in China in 1989.

After that, world events were more interesting to Timmy, as if they had some kind of sport attached to it. He learned geography and was so passionate about it that Bob Costas would soon have had a rival. In Tim's adult years, he slept on the couch a lot because he didn't want to miss his favorite show on ESPN, *Mike and Mike in the Morning*. It was on from 4:00 to 7:00 AM, and yes, I would hear all about it when I got up.

When Timmy was four years old, he was diagnosed with

a kidney problem called nephrotic syndrome, which causes the kidney to become swollen and not process protein properly. His medical issues began with a 10-day stay in the hospital.

There were months when things were very normal; other times, he was very sick. Although he was a smart and active kid at school, it frustrated him that he missed out on so much. He was always the smallest kid, but also the funniest and most charming.

At the age of 12, Tim had his first blood clot. At the age of 19, he diagnosed himself while sitting in his doctor's office. He told Dr. Kahn that the pain in his chest felt like a blood clot; soon after, it was confirmed. At the age of 20, he had a pulmonary embolectomy; it lasted nine painful hours. His heart was kept beating by a bypass machine while the surgeons attempted to scrape out the clot.

The last few years had been difficult for Tim. His bones were bad from years of kidney medicine and his right lung had stopped working completely. Anxiety was a regular part of Timmy's days; only golf or Texas Hold 'Em could keep his mind off of the pain. His heart had to work twice as hard. He so badly wanted for some miracle doctor to fix him, but we never found one.

Many times, while Tim was hospitalized, I would share Scripture with him over the phone. One of my favorites comes from Psalm 61.

"Hear my cry, O God; give heed to my prayer.
From the end of the earth I call to You when my heart is

faint; lead me to the rock that is higher than I.
For You have been a refuge for me,
a tower of strength against the enemy.
— Psalm 61:1-3

Timothy, I know I was not a perfect mom and you were not a perfect son, but I know you knew the perfect God, your Creator. I know you now have a perfect and glorified body.

While you were in your hospital bed in intensive care, you were hallucinating a little bit and you told me that the "pencil sharpener was singing" to you. Before you were hospitalized, you had watched me change the batteries in my pencil sharpener. It came on accidentally and startled you, and we laughed about it. Later, when you told me it was singing, I asked you what song. You sang me the answer.

Amazing grace, how sweet the sound
That saved a wretch like me
I once was lost, but now I'm found
Was blind, but now I see

Timmy, I love you so much. I will miss you every second of every day for the rest of my life. I promise to do my best to turn up the NCAA basketball games loud and follow the tournament. I promise to keep informed on sports statistics. I promise I won't let your brother use your golf clubs.

I would like to thank all of you who have prayed for Timmy and our family through these years, for those who have supported us at the hospital and since his passing. I'd like to give a special thanks to Signature Interiors, Don Lugo High School, and my church, CVCC. We will continue to need your support, for these next days will be hard.

My Timmy has no more pain and God has healed him. I ask the same Lord, the same Comforter, to give us the knowledge that our Timmy is in the ultimate sports arena in heaven, checking all the stats of the latest believers, trying to keep God informed, and making everyone smile. Thank you, God, for the privilege of being Timmy's mom.

~~~

I stepped off the stage with Ted's help, weeping while Amy Lee from Evanescence sang out "My Immortal." The service ended with a beautiful solo of "Amazing Grace" by Kelle Farrell, who was accompanied by Chris Harwood on the piano, both of whose children grew up in the church with Tim.

Tim's life was summarized in a two-hour service. His young life was remembered, funny stories about him were shared, and his pictures were framed. Family and friends gathered from near and far. Condolences and promises were given in cards, words, and hugs. Then they all climbed back into their cars and drove away.

Now what, Lord?

PLAYLIST III

Love Songs

1. "Over the Rainbow" — Israel Kamakawiwo'ole
2. "Now Comes the Night" — Rob Thomas
3. "This is Your Life" — Switchfoot
4. "Winds of Change" — Kutless
5. "Arms of Love" — Kutless
6. "The Reason" — Hoobastank
7. "My Immortal" — Evanescence
8. "Higher" — Creed
9. "Stop This Train" — John Mayer
10. "Legacy" — Kutless
11. "Don't Stop Dancing" — Creed
12. "Til Kingdom Come" — Coldplay

Chapter 12

My Timmy

They call them the "Seven Stages of Grief"—or is it eight? I don't know if I've ever fit into a predictable template. After losing both of my parents (my father while I was in my twenties and my mother seven years before Tim), an ever-changing family dynamic left a thick layer of scar tissue on my grieving heart.

When my dad passed, it manifested itself in a physical way. My hair literally fell out by the handfuls and I was diagnosed with alopecia. After a year of processing, working through the pain of the loss, and meeting with a dermatologist, my hair began to grow back. The unexpected passing of my mother looked much different. Her death left a huge, emotional hole inside of me, along with a large inheritance. I kept myself busy by upgrading my home, taking in several wayward kids, and spoiling my own two.

What would this new grief look like? Would it change me physically, spiritually, emotionally, or psychologically?

There was one thing I knew for sure—I did not want my son to be forgotten. I think every parent who loses a child feels this way. I wanted to talk about Tim. I wanted to talk about God. I wanted God to talk to me continuously. Journaling became my outlet, allowing me to pour out my deepest, most heartfelt grief in words and prayers onto paper. It always brought me into the Lord's presence. When I wrote down my prayers, when I confessed my misgivings, when I acknowledged my own failures, I felt close to God, which also made me feel close to my son. God spoke to me through my own words, boomeranging me back to His love and grace. An insight began to develop within me.

My healing road began here. Slowly, my destination switched from an internal one to an eternal one. Part of me lived with God now, desiring to know Him deeper, to abide in Him, and to experience more of the supernatural. A craving grew inside me, fueling me for the journey ahead. Was it just crazy grief? I didn't have time to analyze myself out of fear that I'd fall back into a dark place. Amazing grace continued and I never wanted to lose sight of it. God's Word seemed to always confirm my feelings and thoughts.

"But as for me, the nearness of God is my good;
I have made the Lord God my refuge,
that I may tell of all Your works."
— Psalm 73:28

Within hours of finishing Tim's service, I sat down at my table and grabbed a new journal. I began to pen a continuation of Tim's eulogy—a poem describing my son, my Timmy.

~~~

My Timmy

My Timmy embraced life
When from pain he was free.
Youthful and idealistic,

Energy like a bee.

Charming and quick
With a wit to tease,
An entertainer he was,
An audience to please.

My Timmy loved life,
Every minute was busy.
His voice filled the air,
A personality that was fizzy.

Bubbling and brewing
With effervescent steam;
You had so much potential,
You did have a dream.

Go to college, of course;
Communications you'd take.
To be a sports analyst, your knowledge
You couldn't fake.

From the Olympics
To World Cup Soccer you knew.
The players, their histories,
Baseball and football too.

But college basketball was
Your favorite sport season.
To be at Duke or UCLA
Would give you good reason,

To jump up and down,

Just be a crazy fan.
Your team spirit was contagious,
Seen in the Chino Football stands.

There are other things you loved,
Your dog, Chance, for one.
He made you laugh
And gave you so much fun.

That big pooch could cuddle
On the couch and not get busted,
Because he was snuggled to you,
His best friend he trusted.

You loved to do stuff
With your Dad by your side.
Helping with hardware at work
Brought you much pride.

That tool belt so cute,
Around your small hips;
But manly you were
With all your drill bits.

You loved your brother, Corey,
When in the womb you did inquire,
"Does the baby have Jesus in his heart?"
Your desire…

To love him unconditionally,
Even twice your size he became.
Your younger "big" brother;
His heart won't be the same.

Timmy loved his Aunt Lauren,
A special bond they did share.
Love of sports and jokes,
Often they would compare.

And the house in Paradise
Where Oma and Opa reside;
A retreat with laughter
And family at your side.

The soccer team was special,
All the boys in red, black, and white.
The memories we'll treasure,
You brought us joy and delight.

My Timmy loved to "party,"
A lot of friends he had.
There is Jody, Susie, and Jennifer,
Across the street, their pad.

Pier fishing and camping,
Or just hanging out,
Timmy, you liked fun,
In this there's no doubt.

Kyle and Kurt, some troubles
You two did stir.
But we love you, you know that,
And Timmy was "cured"…

When he hung out with you guys,

He learned some hard lessons.
Many memories of growing up
And counseling sessions.

Kaycie, Tim wanted
To marry you.
His good friend's sister
And great listener too.

I know he must have
Driven you nuts.
But thanks for your friendship
And patience so much.

Rick, you are special,
A "big brother" you portrayed.
Looking to you for courage
And to be brave.

A few weeks in Tucson;
A chance to be on your own.
Home is where you needed to be;
Your forever comfort zone.

James, Jessica, and Nate
You're also loyal fans,
Of our family forever,
A part of God's plans.

My Timmy was a groupie
Of a band called Solacz.
Sam and boys, you rock
What excitement, that "party bus."

Play a new tune now,
For your number one fan,
An *in-spirit*ational member
Of your infamous rock band.

He loved strawberries and cantaloupe,
Spunky Steer and Round Table,
Del Taco chili cheese fries
And sweet tarts were a staple.

He put sour cream on everything,
Christmas cookies, we'd loved to bake.
Cheesecake and "croquetchas" at New Year's,
Beer at Kelly's and steak.

To sing karaoke
And make the girls laugh,
You loved to entertain,
A great gift to have.

My Timmy loved his game of golf
And quite serious he took it.
The clubs, balls, and clothes,
He never wanted to quit.

Even at times,
He never walked the course.
He relied on the cart,
And that's okay, it's what works.

I know you loved me, Timmy,
Many times did tell

With your hugs and kisses in silence
A bond between us known well.

They told me of frustration,
Forgiveness and hurt.
The tightly held squeeze
Another way to assert.

The words were not spoken
But I know what you felt.
That, my son, always made
My heart melt.

My Timmy, I am sorry
For your pain here on earth.
I am happy though for memories,
And the joy you brought forth.

I will love you forever
And a day on top of that!
Hang out with God now
And to Him, I will chat.

Bring me peace and comfort,
To know you're all right.
Perfect, with a glow
Shining in my heart, so bright.

Love, Mom.

~~~

Timmy was with God now, physically separated from us

on earth and residing in the presence of the Lord. I kept my mind thinking on that, what Tim looked like dancing in heaven without losing breath, his body healed and without blemish. I am reminded of a powerful verse in Romans…

"Who will separate us from the love of Christ? Will tribulation, or distress, or persecution, or famine, or nakedness, or peril, or sword?

Just as it is written, 'For Your sake we are being put to death all day long; we were considered as sheep to be slaughtered.'

But in all these things we overwhelmingly conquer through Him who loved us.

For I am convinced that neither death, nor life, nor angels, nor principalities, nor things present, nor things to come, nor powers, nor height, nor depth, nor any other created thing, will be able to separate us from the love of God, which is in Christ Jesus our Lord."

— Romans 8:35-39

In this verse I placed my hope. I never had to worry about being separated from God's love. My connection to Timmy was both maternal and eternal. It didn't matter that I was sensitive, selfish, insecure, sarcastic, silly, and too serious at times, because I was saved by the sacrifice of a sovereign God who extended His grace through the death of His own Son, Jesus Christ. I accepted Him and my Timmy did as well.

Every believer looks different in their acknowledgment of God's grace, but He loves us all the same. He knows our hearts.

I did not want my grief to damage me to the point where my responsibility for keeping that grace connection alive within me turned messy. The Lord's grace had already brought me to the most authentic place in my life; going backward was not an option. If evil had its way, many destructive things, attitudes, and consequences would bury God's light, but I knew I couldn't survive in the darkness. Grief would not conquer me; I would conquer it. Tim's time had ended on earth, but my time still ticked, and I felt an urgent need to not waste a minute.

My Timmy, how we miss you. My God, My Lord, help me to rest in You this minute...tonight...tomorrow... Awaken me to every reminder that You are with me.

Then, the dreams began.

Chapter 13

Nighttime Counsel

The first dream came only days after Tim's celebration of life. We all dream and can usually only remember bits and pieces. However, I awoke and could remember it all. I quickly wrote it all down before I could forget. As I wrote, everything made sense in my head. I felt a deeper connection to God, like He was explaining a level of my soul within my unconscious mind in order to help me further grasp my grief. It was like reading a long novel and knowing that there would be some hard chapters, but the ending would clear everything up and the heroine would succeed. I closed my journal and hoped for a sequel.

In the first dream, it seemed like a completely normal day. I was driving with someone through the canyon near my home, but I didn't know who the passenger was. It was a generic face, neither male nor female. All I knew was that I felt as comfortable with this person as I would a friend. We looked out at the hills and chatted away. We talked about the upcoming spring, noticing how the landscape was beginning to show signs of change. The winter brown was turning to the green of early spring throughout the pastures and rolling hills of the familiar canyon.

Suddenly, the car left the road.

We flew through the air, soaring over the valley below. My hands firmly gripped the steering wheel as I tried not to panic. I was optimistic that all would be okay; I reassured the person next to me. I moved the steering wheel and realized it was acting like a boat rudder. If I turned it the right way, the wind would catch it and glide us down gently to safety. We continued to sail and the ground loomed closer.

We never crashed and there was no violent end to the dream, yet I experienced a rush of adrenaline in my stomach and I bucked against the feeling of not being in control. I felt a sense of responsibility for the person sitting in the car next to me, that whatever decision I made on this "flight" would directly impact them as well.

As I wrote down the details of my dream, I felt so many things. I experienced an excitement that the dream held meaning, one I believed I would come to understand as I wrote it all down. I knew the car leaving the road and flying through the air conveyed a sense of loss of control. As a woman and as a mom, I wanted to be in control, yet I couldn't cure my own son. When he became an adult and his health issues ramped up, the decisions being made by medical professionals and government agencies brought me frustration.

When we launched off the road, I realized we had two options—crash or land safely. As we sat suspended in the air, I believe the Lord spoke to me that He remains in control. He asked me to turn toward the wind. The promise of spring in my dream gave me hope. I knew that something new and promised was coming.

I wanted to steer the uncontrollable toward a soft landing. However, as hard as I tried, my "steering" didn't change anything. God had asked me to turn toward the wind, which I knew represented His Holy Spirit, and I did. I was carried to safety because I trusted God.

I also felt unsettled as I wrote down my dream, mostly because of the person in the car with me. I didn't know if that very calm entity was Timmy or Jesus or someone completely different. He or she seemed to represent something more abstract to me—eternity. God communicated to me as I wrote; it was my responsibility to bow down to Him and pray that I might reach the point of acceptance. I needed to live in and hope for greener hills. My truth had crumpled and dented my heart. I felt many mixed emotions of regret, knowing that I could turn my dream into either a rescue operation or another fatality.

Every morning I woke up, I was faced with a decision to make. Most mornings I couldn't see clearly through my grief. Nevertheless, grace and comfort gathered around me every day. I wondered if my dreams would be a constant thing.

One day I wrote in my journal, *"In joyous exultation, this 'friend' commented on the beauty of the newly green hills with a big smile..."*

Eternity—a place to steer my heart toward. I prayed for God to bring me more hope and direction in my dreams.

"He is before all things,
and in Him all things hold together."
— Colossians 1:17

The second dream was much more complicated than the first. Still, I remembered every detail and wrote it all down in my mourning of the morning.

In the dream, Ted and I sat in the waiting room at a hospital and a lot of people were gathered around us. A doctor came out and gave us a diagnosis for Tim—autism. We immediately began calling our friends and family, sharing the news. Then we got into our car and turned onto the freeway to drive home. I recognized the freeway as the one near the house I grew up in. As we drove home, our gas gauge read empty. We were unprepared and out of money. I called my dear friend, Lynn, who lived close by. She was very eager to help us out. Ted veered the car toward the exit for Lynn's house but missed it. We continued on the freeway to the next exit, but we suddenly realized that something was terribly wrong. As we attempted to exit the freeway, we saw four cars driving *up* the off-ramp. Ted swerved the car to get around them and they continued onto the freeway going the wrong way. The dream ended there.

As I wrote about the dream where we sat in the waiting room with several people gathered around us, I felt as though it was a metaphor for life—we wait, we hope, and we do it best when we are surrounded by community. We would never be alone if we had the body of Christ near us. God had blessed us abundantly with people in our lives that loved Him and wanted to support us; I knew this from experience.

"As each one has received a special gift, employ it in serving one another as good stewards of the manifold grace of God."
— 1 Peter 4:10

I came to the conclusion that the doctor's diagnosis of autism represented a condition for myself as well as Tim. I was unable to truly communicate all of my jumbled thoughts; I simply wrote in the moment, placing my thoughts and dreams in these sacred pages. I hoped by writing it all down I would receive some clarity, for I had experienced that before when I wrote in my journals.

Is there any organization to grief?

I was also no longer able to communicate with Tim in a physical sense. Often, kids with autism struggle to make eye contact during conversations, which I believe was another metaphor for earthly separation. I worked very closely with special needs kids, so I was familiar with the spectrum.

Lynn represented a specific support from someone who had also experienced the loss of a child. Our friendship had a deep foundation in faith, and she remained a constant support during this season. When we missed the off-ramp, I related that to my earnest praying for the miraculous healing of our son. I wanted to accept that God had a different way, a plan beyond what I could see. I hoped He would pave a route where all things would be made clear in His timing. I needed to trust His way, not my own.

At the next exit, four cars sped the wrong way against the normal flow of traffic. Four was a very specific number that represented the four individuals in the VanTilburg family, each of which had a car with a personal license plate. I prayed we would travel together and not take such different ways through this grief, down roads that never connected again. I knew that God had to be the bridge which connected us to healing, to eternity, and to more of His grace. We needed to find that placed called "Joy" once again.

I prayed these prayers, thought these thoughts, and watched as the words spread across the pages of my journal. I penned a heartfelt question before closing it… *"Would we each be willing to see what lies ahead and trust Him in the traffic of oncoming life?"*

For now, I needed a designated driver, and the Lord's grace confirmed this in my heart as tears continued to stain each page.

"I will bless the Lord who has counseled me;
indeed, my mind instructs me in the night."
— Psalm 16:7

Chapter 14

His Perfect Will

I took three more weeks off before going back to work. In that time, I listened to music every night to fall asleep, thankful for the invention of the iPod. I wrote a ton of "thank you" cards in an attempt to function and stay busy. I felt restlessness in every muscle and nerve ending.

Normal things, like going to the grocery store or looking into my dog's face (who somehow seemed to understand my pain), set the tears off. I couldn't walk down the grocery store aisle where they shelved canned ravioli because Tim loved those. People and their impatience with their children in public gave me anxiety. I'd look at strangers and wonder how everyone just kept doing what they were doing when I felt as though I was drowning. The "what ifs" and the "how comes" started conversing in my head. Ted and I talked briefly about it, but it became too painful. He felt it too.

I thought a lot about my aunt Dolores. She suffered from the same grief which was plaguing me—she lost a son to disease in his early adulthood. I was 19 years old at the time. I remember my cousin, Raymond, well; he and I were the same age, only six months apart. Bone cancer cut away at his young life. Although the details of my aunt's stages of grief were kept within the more "adult circles" of the family, I knew that she physically took herself into a dark place, literally hiding under her house. She was rescued by my uncle and spent some time being emotionally nurtured in a "special hospital." What didn't make sense to me at 19, I now completely understood, for grief leads one to the edge. The desire to crawl on my belly to a dark place and hide from my life's reality grew within me; I felt its pull. I even remember asking Ted to cover up the table with a blanket so I couldn't see the space underneath.

Intent on becoming intentional in my healing, and in seeking and understanding the purposes of God, I prayed for God to show me His presence. If that meant having a hyper-diligence in searching and seeking God in everything, and doing the same in writing everything down, I was fine having that become my own "crazy."

God brought a wise woman to counsel me on this very thing. We talked about God's sovereignty. I'd always heard that word, but I didn't quite think on it or get it too much until our conversations began. I knew what it meant; God, the project manager, CEO, controller, supreme king of His children, reigns above all. Tim had sung "Amazing Grace" in his last chorus of words to me, giving me peace to know that God had ushered him into paradise. I wasn't stressing over that part… No, this was about me. Why was this God's purpose for me?

The sovereign God is perfect, holy, and just. I believed that for Tim, now I needed to believe it for myself. God, accomplishing His will in Timmy, received my son unto Himself. I was not to question God's intent, but to seek His will for me through this tragedy.

We are all clay in the potter's hands. Whatever He makes of us is to complete His perfect will. Why did God think I'd be worthy of surviving this? Was it some kind of punishment?

I reflected on a familiar passage from Scripture…

"And we know that God causes all things to work together for good to those who love God, to those who are called according to His purpose."
— *Romans 8:28*

It was that word again—trust. God seemed to be trying to plant this word into my heart.

Use a gentle hand trowel, God, not a jackhammer!

I read His Word a lot. With the Holy Spirit ministering to me, I started to let go of the guilt, the "what ifs," the "should've," and the "could've." Destructive thoughts served only to bind me from grasping the healing God had for me. Being held captive not only hurt me, but it stifled my progress. I wanted to thrive and work out His plan. His amazing grace softly troweled the soil of my doubts, planting even more hope and understanding within.

God is gentle and merciful. He took Timmy to heaven and ended his suffering, but His plan would continue on with my family and me. Sovereignty meant God was in control, not me.

"Seek the Lord while He may be found; call upon Him while He is near.

Let the wicked forsake his way and the unrighteous man his

thoughts; and let him return to the Lord,
and He will have compassion on him, and to our God, for
He will abundantly pardon.

'For My thoughts are not your thoughts, nor are your ways
My ways,' declares the Lord.

'For as the heavens are higher than the earth,
so are My ways higher than your ways and My thoughts
than your thoughts.

For as the rain and the snow come down from heaven, and
do not return there without watering the earth and making
it bear and sprout, and furnishing seed to the sower and
bread to the eater; so will My word be which goes forth
from My mouth; it will not return to Me empty, without
accomplishing what I desire, and without succeeding in the
matter for which I sent it.

For you will go out with joy and be led forth with peace;
the mountains and the hills will break forth into shouts of
joy before you,
and all the trees of the field will clap their hands.

Instead of the thorn bush the cypress will come up, and
instead of the nettle the myrtle will come up, and it will be a
memorial to the Lord, for an everlasting sign which will not
be cut off.'"

— Isaiah 55:6-13

I felt a sense of responsibility, like a field chosen for a certain type of crop. I didn't know what to expect, but I wanted God's desired purpose to grow from the clay of my life. I didn't want to wait for the winds of grief to blow away the topsoil. Spring was just around the corner and I longed for the warmth of the sun. Staying busy with the right things became essential in my process of healing. Even still, I was heartbroken, crying for my loss and missing my son every morning, afternoon, and especially in the evening.

PLAYLIST IV

Life Songs

1. "Could It Be Any Harder" — The Calling
2. "Goodbye for Now" — P.O.D.
3. "Somewhere I Belong" — Linkin Park
4. "Be Yourself" — Audioslave
5. "If You Could See Me Now" — P.O.D.
6. "Atmosphere" — TobyMac
7. "Whenever I Say Your Name" — Sting (feat. Mary J. Blige)
8. "Walk On" — U2
9. "I Just Love You" — Five for Fighting
10. "Afterglow" — INXS
11. "Breathing" — Lifehouse
12. "Calling All Angels" — Train
13. "Father, Spirit, Jesus" — Casting Crowns
14. "And Now My Lifesong Sings" — Casting Crowns

Chapter 15

Playing Through

"And I heard a voice from heaven, like the sound of many waters and like the sound of loud thunder, and the voice which I heard was like the sound of harpists playing on their harps."
— Revelation 14:2

Clink-clink, clank-clank…
Clink-clank, clink-clank…
Clinkety, clinkety, clinkety…
Crrrrrr-thump!
Clank, clank, clank…

Harp music… I knew that's what I heard! You may not recognize it as such, but I knew these chords. I felt it coming from somewhere, maybe heaven.

Back at work, in a high school classroom, I sat catching up on my notes before class started. I was glad to be back in the swing of things, at least attempting anyway. Getting back into a familiar routine helped after a three-week absence. There were no "Timmy memories" at my job and I didn't think I'd be caught off guard there. However, my senses were engaged more than I knew, and I could hear them in the distance, the sound growing louder.

I knew that sound—the sound of someone carrying golf clubs. Whoever it was plopped the bag of clubs onto the floor; the metal hit against each other, rattling in the bag. Tim loved golf. The times he was able to play were times when he was freed from worrying about his health. When he came home after, he never left his clubs outside. He would walk in the front door with the bag slung over his arm, the clubs rattling, clinkety-clanking, and crrrrrr-thumping in his bag in the middle of the living room floor. His face was always flushed, and he was smiling as he announced his (probably embellished) game and the people he met out on the course.

The floodgates of my brain opened; I expected to look up from my desk and see Timmy coming through the door with his "instruments" slung over his shoulder.

The teacher's room where I sat also served as the headquarters for the school's golf team. That day, though, it became a music room. A player walked in to deposit his clubs. As if in slow motion, the sounds reacted in my brain. Tears welled up and began to drain down my face. My focus was suddenly lost. I once again experienced joy at hearing the "clinkety-clank," yet there was a profound sadness knowing that Timmy and his clubs were not present. The sound swung hard at my heart, and I had to rely on the Holy Spirit to caddy me. I needed to embrace the moment, the first hole of many on this course of grief, while also attempting to get back to living, loving, and aiming toward more grace moments.

I was caught in the debris, the sounds swirling around me. It was a swift whirlpool. I knew these sounds would forever trigger a memory. I'd hear them again from Ted and Corey; both of them enjoyed golf and had played with Tim often. I knew they would want to play again in order to honor him, walking the same course, holding the same clubs, laughing and crying over old memories. I, too, needed to stay away from letting a sand trap or water hazard memory turn into a bogey.

This sound, the "clinkety-clank," like harps from heaven, reminded me of my Master. Writing down memories turned them into gifts from the Lord, like adding up my scorecard. Whether par for the course or a mulligan, I wanted to keep playing straight through, no matter how hazardous some days might be. I trusted in my Master's plan.

"And they sang a new song before the throne…"
— Revelation 14:3

~~~

The days moved along and soon the calendar turned to late April, then on to May. Ted's birthday and my birthday are only a week apart. Birthdays, as indicated in the very name, mark a *birth*, the celebration that a life began. However, the mood to celebrate seemed uncomfortable, bringing only pain.

I jotted this prayer-poem down in my journal.

~~~

Birthday Blues

Today is my birthday,
Not such good news.

Another year older,
I've surely paid my dues.

Why am I another year here?
When the son I loved
Could not finish
And be near?

But instead I will remember
This precious gift I had
And being your mom.
On this day I am sad.

Please help me Lord
To get through this day
Surround me with love
And friends who do pray.

Birthday blues,
Sunrise hues;
A promise praise
In all of my days.

Amen.

~~~

Playing through these days and the holidays to come presented a formidable challenge. Some things would never be the same. Ted found so much comfort in music; I embraced the lyrics and tunes, but I hoped for something more…more of God in my every waking moment.

Corey began moving in deliberate strides to correct the wayward things in his life. This made me so proud. Encouragement from dear friends literally turned his life toward the promise of a successful future. He dotted all the *i*'s and crossed all the *t*'s, so to speak, and stepped up to adulthood. He didn't talk much about his brother or his feelings (and still doesn't to this day), but every once in a while, I'd see him encouraging a friend on Facebook. I knew his heart was caring and empathetic. He totally took up the mantle of his brother's golf game. He held very special memories by playing the game that his big brother introduced him to. I knew Tim would be proud of the way Corey played through the rough, always landing on the green.

"For I am confident of this very thing, that He who began a good work in you will perfect it until the day of Christ Jesus. For it is only right for me to feel this way about you all, because I have you in my heart..."
— Philippians 1:6-7

PLAYLIST V

Grace

1. "Animal I Have Become" — Three Days Grace
2. "Move Along" — The All-American Rejects
3. "The Real Life" — 3 Doors Down
4. "Wake Me Up When September Ends" — Green Day
5. "Oh My God" — Jars of Clay
6. "Feel the Silence" — The Goo Goo Dolls
7. "Without You Here" — The Goo Goo Dolls
8. "A Message" — Coldplay
9. "God Will Lift Up Your Head" — Jars of Clay
10. "Daylight" — Coldplay
11. "On Fire" — Switchfoot
12. "Praise You in This Storm" — MercyMe
13. "God Put a Smile upon Your Face" — Coldplay
14. "Take Me Higher" — Jars of Clay
15. "I'll Fly Away" — Jars of Clay
16. "I Can Only Imagine" — MercyMe

Chapter 16

Consider It All

"Consider it all joy, my brethren, when you encounter various trials, knowing that the testing of your faith produces endurance.

And let endurance have its perfect result, so that you may be perfect and complete, lacking in nothing.

But if any of you lacks wisdom, let him ask of God, who gives to all generously and without reproach, and it will be given to him."

— James 1:2-5

Consider... The Merriam-Webster dictionary defines this word as "thinking carefully about; regarding or treating in an attentive or kindly way," especially as it concerns making a decision or judgment.

In its imperative form, the word challenged me to take my trials and turn them into joy. I related it to the Pythagorean theorem, you know...$a^2+b^2=c^2$. According to James 1, I had a new formula...*trials and testing + hope and faith = perfect wisdom and joy.* I didn't always have a calculator on me, I used a lot of scratch paper, and I needed tutoring and a big eraser. However, I learned that through taking steps closer to Him, on both the good days and the bad, faith would be produced within me.

Could I navigate through this chapter without failure?

I had a friend whose career was in marriage and family counseling. He came alongside me and offered his time as a service to me. He told me that he was available for as long as I needed to chat. All I needed to do was give his office a call. What a blessing! I hoped Ted and Corey would join me in these conversations, or at least would consider it.

Four years prior to Tim's passing, our family unexpectedly lost our home to a fire. Those were extremely hard days. I sat down and considered those events, likening them to an algebra problem. At the time, of course, I thought I was barely making the grade. I knew I did not want to become a statistic. I read through some old journals, pondering those days after the fire.

It became clear, an epiphany, like somehow the rubble had been swept away. God highlighted to me that those hard, cleansing days had reconnected me to Him. He was preparing me for this time. He asked me to trust Him then, knowing I would need to trust Him even more so now. Scripture always reiterated what God spoke to me in my heart.

"Before I was afflicted I went astray,
but now I keep Your word.
You are good and do good; teach me Your statues."
— Psalm 119:67-68

As I recalled and reread the prayers, promises, and verses I'd placed my hope in years before, I started to hear God more intimately, even more personally than I ever had in all my years of saving grace. My family had been displaced from comfort, and I had become lonely and fearful, living in unfriendly places. I found my shelter in Him; He became my true refuge. Like David, I named my dwelling place while in that time of transition "The Cave." Deep in the darkness of the unknown, I became my truest self with God Almighty. Now, in even more intense heartache and uncertainty, I couldn't go back to faking it.

After connecting the two events—my house burning down and my son passing away—I saw the vast measure of God's grace along His timeline. I saw how the fire became "holy ground" for the work He did in my heart. God continued to minister to me through the fire, though we had long since moved past those days. For the first time, I thanked Him for that eventful day. I wasn't thankful for the flames, mind you, but for all I had gleaned from the ashes. I suddenly became very aware that the firestorm in my life was meant to prepare me spiritually and emotionally for such a time as this. The purpose of that fire, though horrific and heartbreaking, resulted in the restoration of my faith. That hurt, fear, and loss gave me the strength to remain standing. What I had learned and treasured in my heart then, all the strength I acquired, would now serve to carry me through this new time of mourning. It would allow me to see God's sovereign plan at work.

I moved through the steps of my spiritual algebra problem, lingering for a while in the b^2 part—hope and faith. God was showing me every single day that His calculations would always result in absolute truth.

"I am the way, and the truth, and the life…"
— John 14:6

In this grief, God remodeled my heart and called me worthy. He found me worthy enough to die on a cross for; He was crucified for all my unworthiness. He found me worthy to be Timmy's mother. He found me worthy, revealing His glory through the windowpanes of my sorrows. His sovereignty cleared the way to see into the edge of eternity. As I prayed, I asked Him to show me every bit of it, to show me how to live in it, to continue to rebuild past the mantle of mourning and onto the rooftop of revelation.

God is omniscient—all-knowing. My mind was boggled to think that He knew exactly how I would react in these days. I was constantly reminded that He was the great architect. In all my imperfections, God's grace covered me like cement on a new slab; He poured His grace into my "cave," providing a foundation for me to stand firmly upon. He gave me the tools and the strength to continue on. My prayer every minute was to keep my focus on Him, with a searched, cleansed, and ready heart.

"O Lord, You have searched me and known me.
You know when I sit down and when I rise up;
You understand my thought from afar.
You scrutinize my path and my lying down, and are
intimately acquainted with all my ways.
Even before there is a word on my tongue,
behold, O Lord, You know it all.
You have enclosed me behind and before,
and laid Your hand upon me.
Such knowledge is too wonderful for me;

it is too high, I cannot attain to it."
— Psalm 139:1-6

I pulled out a notebook from the previous year and flipped to a study I did in the book of James. I was learning to "consider." It was a work of something greater. Everything became spiritual to me. I had a keen sense of the Holy Spirit actively invading my thoughts. It was like I was viewing life through a kaleidoscope of God moments; a beautiful picture of words was projected onto the pages when I wrote. Writing helped me understand what was going on in my own heart. Prayer gave me the insight to continue to see. A small but mighty verse took precedence in my heart.

"Cease striving and know that I am God…"
— Psalm 46:10

After Timmy's passing, the reality of this only intensified for me. I asked my counselor about it because it sometimes overwhelmed me. I needed his expertise on what was healthy thinking and what was not. I continued to think deeply on it, seeing and hearing the spiritual in almost everything.

"Do you think it is a blessing or a curse?" my grief counselor asked me after I described the thoughts and supernatural insight I was experiencing.

Intimacy with the Lord made me feel close to Timmy… How could that ever be a curse?

My counselor believed, as did I, that the Holy Spirit was being magnified within me because I had fully surrendered to Him. Once again, I was being lavished with grace upon amazing grace. I continued to build on the trust I put in the Lord and considered my own purpose as wholly for His kingdom.

Chapter 17

Bittersweet

The middle of May brought with it a celebration of mothers. There was nothing extraordinary about that day, except that there was a hyper-focus on the idea of mothers and their children—a very loud, in-your-face type of reality that year. With my certain sensitivity, the air became palpable. It was as though all anybody could see was my tragedy. I was the mother of a dear son named Corey, but when I was asked, I would always say that I was the mother of two boys.

Good friends took us to lunch after church that day. We received some cards in the mail and flowers on our doorstep. Not only was I struggling as a mother who had lost her son, but I also missed my own mother. I stayed up late, well after 10:00 PM. The house was quiet, and I needed time to reflect.

The sweetest blessing came beeping into my silence late that night. It was a text message that read "Happy Mother's Day." I didn't recognize the number it was sent from. I inquired who the mystery sender was. She replied with her name—Tiana, a childhood friend of Tim's. She wasn't able to attend his service, so I had sent her a memorial program and a few pictures.

I finally turned my phone off and resolved to put that bittersweet day behind me, only to return to my journal in the morning and compose a poem-prayer about the emotional weekend.

~~~

Text Message to a Mom

Bittersweet day
Missing my son,
Dreading these hours
Of Mother's Day to come.

Started late, Saturday night
Tears flow
Listening to music
Tim and I know.

Went to worship, Lord,
Corey by my side.
I'm glad for his choice
Setting aside his pride.

Lunch a sure treat
With dear friends we enjoy
A beautiful afternoon,
But still miss my boy.

Cards, flowers from friends,
Hugs and kisses too.
Missing my mom;
Two reasons to feel blue.

It's 10:30 at night
Cell phone sends a beep.

A text message from someone;
It sounded so sweet.

"Happy Mother's Day," it said.
"I'll be calling you soon.
But sending X's, O's."
To assume…

I'd know who sent it,
But I did not believe,
I recognized the number
On the screen I see.

So, I text back to the sender,
"Thank you, but who is this from?"
"I'm sorry," the words appear,
"It's Tiana, Timmy's old chum."

"I received Tim's memorial you sent,
Of which I am grateful.
It made me sad 2 see it,
All these years…so painful."

"Those pix I enjoyed,
Remember him so well.
But you are his mom and
You loved him so much, I can tell."

Timmy, I wish I could
Just send you a text,
See how you are,
When I'll see you next.

Text me back please,
Some X's and O's.
I'll wait for the beep
Of love you compose.

Love, Mom

~~~

*"Blessed be the God and Father of our Lord Jesus Christ,
who according to His great mercy has caused us to be born
again to a living hope through the resurrection of Jesus
Christ from the dead, to obtain an inheritance which is
imperishable and undefiled and will not fade away,
reserved in heaven for you, who are protected by the power
of God through faith for a salvation ready to be revealed in
the last time."*
— 1 Peter 1:3-5

Corey continued down a positive path. He completed a few credits and received his high school diploma. He then applied for the ITT Technical Institute. His senior year of high school had been compromised by the fire and so much emotional turmoil, causing my youngest son to fall behind. Now it was the first week of June, Friday the 8th, and we had an appointment to pick up his diploma from the adult school in our town. He was scheduled to start his first day at ITT Tech on the following Monday.

I left work early that Friday morning to swing by the house and pick Corey up. That's when God's angels pushed the right people in just the right places to give us a huge blessing! The principal at Corey's high school *just happened* to be the principal of the adult school as well. He greeted us as we walked into the office. Insistent that Corey have his own personal graduation ceremony, he set the wheels in motion, grabbing a cap and gown for both himself and Corey. Another one of our close friends who had supported us throughout the years and even taught Corey *just happened* to be in the neighborhood. He came across the street to congratulate Corey and ended up in the ceremony himself after being provided a cap and gown. The receptionist left her desk to take pictures of Corey as he was presented with his diploma. "Pomp and Circumstance" played in the background.

That's not even the best part! We found out later that we didn't even have an appointment! Neither the principal nor our friend had any idea about this, but God certainly did, and He worked it out for Corey's good.

Despite all of the focus on what we'd lost, Corey exemplified hope and perseverance. That Friday served as a glorious step toward my youngest son gaining his own independence. I knew that God not only heard my prayers but wanted to answer them!

"And we desire that each one of you show the same diligence so as to realize the full assurance of hope until the end..."
— Hebrews 6:11

"Blessed is a man who perseveres under trial; for once he has been approved, he will receive the crown of life which the Lord has promised to those who love Him."
— James 1:12

PLAYLIST VI

Believe

1. "I Miss You" — Incubus
2. "Bleeds Like Me" — Trapt
3. "Nothing Else Matters" — Metallica
4. "We Believe" — Good Charlotte
5. "Hold On" — Good Charlotte
6. "How to Save a Life" — The Fray
7. "Boston" — Augustana
8. "Stay" — 12 Stones
9. "Take My Hand" — Shawn McDonald
10. "Paradise" — Bruce Springsteen
11. "Split Screen Sadness" — John Mayer
12. "Wheel" — John Mayer
13. "The Face of Love" — Sanctus Real
14. "Word of God Speak" — MercyMe
15. "Drive" — Incubus
16. "I Miss You" (acoustic) — Incubus

Chapter 18

Of Heartbeats and Beasts

After leaving our little apartment behind, we moved into a rental house. It was difficult to live in an apartment for various reasons, but one of the main difficulties was that our 12-year-old dog, Chance, lost his freedom to romp and play outside. At our new house, he was filled with newfound life. He loved our family dearly and seemed to miss Timmy as much as we did. In times of tears, he cuddled right up close, laying his big head and jowls on our thighs, breathing heavy sighs.

On June 19, in the middle of an unrelenting heat spell, Ted called me from work. He said he felt nauseous and dizzy, and he complained that his heartbeat "felt funny." He left work halfway through the day and drove two hours home. When he arrived, I took him straight to the ER in town. He was assessed by Dr. Diaz, one of Timmy's favorite ER doctors.

"How's your son doing?" he asked us.

We repeated the story in default mode. The reaction was surreal. I watched as the strong ER doctor and his nurses, who cared for Timmy so many times, teared up and left the room, overwhelmed with emotion. Even the nutritionist heard and came to find us, expressing her sympathies for our loss.

Ted's heartbeat skipped and bounced; mine did too.

He received his diagnosis—AFib, Atrial fibrillation, a flutter or abnormal heartbeat, when the electrical impulse of the heart is no longer normal.

We knew.

"The pattern is off..."

We knew.

"As a result, your heart cannot pump enough blood to meet your body's needs..."

We knew... Ted had a broken heart.

He stayed that night and the next in the hospital. Physically, Ted was stabilized, but his heart would never be the same.

Our dog was waiting in the driveway when I pulled in. He knew Timmy had left one night and never came back; he sensed my grief. I pulled him in by his leash and he lay by the front door. I held the phone up to his ear so Ted could assure him that he was okay.

"...and hope does not disappoint, because the love of God has been poured out within our hearts through the Holy Spirit who was given to us."
— Romans 5:5

Ted needed a big dose of heart medicine, the kind given

by the one true Healer of our wounds— the Great Physician.
I believe Ted filled the prescription.

~~~

Tim's death happened in the eighth month of our year
lease. By the end of May—almost 11 months in—our
landlord gave us notice that we'd have to move again. He
cited no reason and granted no mercy.

~~~

We Moved Again...

We moved again,
Fourth time in four years.
In each place
A lot of tears.

A fire is what started it all.
But actually, God,
I see Your purpose,
Your higher call.

A motel, just a shelter,
An apartment...
Our stuff, our lives,
Helter-skelter.

A house to rent,
Never felt like home.
A year though not forgotten;
Grief, comfort, friendships, and poems.

Timmy is home,
Of that I am sure.
For us, I pray that in God
Is where we rest and feel secure.

~~~

"...for in Him we live and move and exist, as even some of our own poets have said, 'For we also are his children.'"
— *Acts 17:28*

God's providence went before us. The rental house was not a healthy place for our family and God Himself moved us out. Through some friends, we found a cute townhouse just a mile down the road. Our dog, however, decided it was time for him to settle in for good. Like in the movie *Marley and Me*, Chance took himself for a walk away from the house. Ted finally found him and made the sad assessment that we were about to experience another bout of heartbreak. Chance never moved to the townhouse with us. We stopped what we were doing and the three of us spent several quiet hours comforting and loving Chance in the remaining moments of his life.

Chance... A big, lovable beast of a dog, with such a smile and such an appetite! He was strong, loyal, trustworthy, beautiful, and smart. His eyes shifted to each of us, relaying his love for us. We lavished our love and gratitude on him for what he meant to us. I knew he understood our words. He was ready to go and find Timmy in heaven's fields. We again let our hearts fly to God as we kissed that furry face and black nose goodbye.

Poetic thoughts continued to fill the pages in my journal.

~~~

From Chance

You fed me when I was hungry,
You kept water in my dish.
You let me sleep on anything,
Or in any place I wished.

You sometimes let me lick your hands,
Or even kiss your face.
Despite the fact I've licked myself,
In every sort of place.

You taught me how to come when called.
You taught me how to sit.
You always let me go outside,
So I could take a…stroll.

About that night when love called…
Sorry Timmy, you chased me shoeless,
Around the block and school.
That sticker weed was ruthless!

I remember your return to
The house with no roof.
We all slept in the cold,
Warmed by our love, the proof.

You took me in,

When I went astray.
I left for a while but
I came back to stay.

There is pizza in heaven,
Chocolate chewy bars too.
I received a jeweled collar...
Timmy and I wait for you.

~~~

The very first pet I lost and grieved over was a parakeet named Newton. I was in the fifth grade. There was a specific verse that brought comfort to me. God placed animals and pets in our lives for a reason, to teach and show us unconditional love and compassion. They bring great comfort and joy, and they trust in us as we trust in our Master.

"But now ask the beasts, and let them teach you;
and the birds of the heavens, and let them tell you.
Or speak to the earth, and let it teach you;
and let the fish of the sea declare to you."
— Job 12:7-8

PLAYLIST VII

Home

1. "Lost!" — Coldplay
2. "Jai Ho! (You Are My Destiny)" — A. R. Rahman & The Pussycat Dolls (feat. Nicole Scherzinger)
3. "The Motions" — Matthew West
4. "Give Me Your Eyes" — Brandon Heath
5. "Believe" — Staind
6. "By Your Side" — Tenth Avenue North
7. "There Will Be a Day" — Jeremy Camp
8. "Cinderella" — Steven Curtis Chapman
9. "Amazing Grace (My Chains Are Gone)" — Chris Tomlin
10. "Breathe" — Michael W. Smith
11. "Healing Hand of God" — Jeremy Camp
12. "I'm Alive" — Jeremy Camp
13. "I Do Not Belong" — Kutless
14. "My Heart Will Fly" — MercyMe
15. "Finally Home" — MercyMe
16. "This Is Home" — Switchfoot

Chapter 19

Flight Plan

We packed up and further prepared for our move. It was not only physically challenging, but also spiritually taxing. For the first time in four years, we actually had all our stuff with us and out of storage. The weather was stifling, and Ted's health instructions were clear. His activities were to remain "low stress." It took us over a week to get it all done.

After his passing, we hadn't packed up any of Tim's things. Now, we were forced to deal with it all. I remember that hour, walking into Tim's bedroom in total silence. Ted and I both were crying as we packed away his clothes, personal things, and memories in boxes to take to our new house.

We need to move again,
Dad and I stand at your door.
We face your belongings,
Now meaning so much more.

I pack it up now,
For you have moved along.
Your comfort's in heaven
Memories, now to us belong.

Souvenirs, treasures, collectibles, equipment, clothes, and keepsakes…

A trophy from a winning baseball team... Another from a soccer team he never should have been on, but grace and friendship made room...

Boxes and boxes of baseball cards...

Golf tees and balls, small green pencils and golf shoes...

A tiny statue of a Chinese man fishing that Tim's grandma gave him...

Scooby-Doo pajama bottoms given to him by a friend...

A small water fountain to listen to at night...

Books, CDs, "get well soon" cards...

All the wind-up toys I used to bring him when he was in the hospital...

Hats and more hats... Oh, how he loved his caps!

I picked up his New Testament Bible. It was as though he said, "Please keep my stuff, Mom. You know I'm with you."

We have all your stuff, Tim. We'll keep it close in sight. But you, Son, is what we'll hold onto forever in our hearts.

His things remained packed. Eventually, we gave away most of his clothes, and his golf equipment was distributed between Ted and Corey.

Meanwhile, my Creator continued to transform my

broken heart. I wrote in my journal, "I know, Lord, I have the hope and promise of knowing You as my Savior. You moved us so that I might get a new perspective on things…on Your purpose."

God, in His mercy, awakened me to His morning light so that I could see His hand in the wind of the trees. I took in the very breath of His mercy and comfort. Dawn beckoned me and, through the tears of grief and through the music of my soul, God prepared a gift that would come to define my healing process.

"Therefore, brethren, be all the more diligent to make
certain about His calling and choosing you;
for as long as you practice these things, you will never
stumble; for in this way the entrance into the eternal
kingdom of our Lord and Savior Jesus Christ will be
abundantly supplied to you.

Therefore, I will always be ready to remind you of these
things, even though you already know them,
and have been established in the truth
which is present with you.

I consider it right, as long as I am in this earthly dwelling,
to stir you up by way of reminder…"

— 2 Peter 1:10-13

~~~

Traffic control sent an all-clear for takeoff. I waited in the wings, a clear view of the tarmac. Dawn approached. The flight attendants primped and donned their uniforms. The pilot went over his checklist and flight manifest, preparing for takeoff. I climbed aboard.

PLAYLIST VIII

Restoration

1. "With Arms Wide Open" — Creed
2. "Your Song" — Elton John
3. "Love of My Life" — Santana (feat. Dave Matthews and Carter Beauford)
4. "Waiting On the World to Change" — John Mayer
5. "When I Look to the Sky" — Train
6. "All Because of You" — U2
7. "You Raise Me Up" — Selah
8. "Wherever You Will Go" — The Calling
9. "You're Missing" — Bruce Springsteen
10. "View from Heaven" — Yellowcard
11. "When You Are Near" — Jeremy Camp
12. "Set Me Free" — Casting Crowns
13. "Word of God Speak" — Kutless
14. "Restored" — Jeremy Camp
15. "Praise You in This Storm" — Casting Crowns
16. "I Need Thee Every Hour" — Jars of Clay

Chapter 20

Sunrise Swallowtails
(A Time and a Purpose unto Heaven)

The move took place on the first week of July. I was off contract with my job and summer was upon us. Our new house was replete with freshly painted walls and a tree-lined street that was populated with playing children—all boys. I had idle time now to get used to our "new normal," trying to do ordinary things in a straitjacket of hurt.

"What advantage does man have in all his work which he
does under the sun?
A generation goes and a generation comes,
but the earth remains forever.
Also, the sun rises and the sun sets;
and hastening to its place it rises there again."
— Ecclesiastes 1:3-5

So much busyness swirled around in my mind. My sleep patterns were totally out of whack and I often woke up in the dark, around 4:30 in the morning. I discovered a community park just two houses down. Huge pine and sycamore trees stood guard over the path that wound around the pool and clubhouse. Lights secured the view, beaming off the walkway. I grabbed my music and tied up my tennis shoes, sliding out the door in the dark. I walked, cried, prayed, and listened to music...listened for God.

"There is an appointed time for everything.
And there is a time for every event under heaven..."
— Ecclesiastes 3:1

Around and around the park I walked. Sometimes I counted the laps... 18, 19, 20... Other times I listened to music and sang in the silence of pre-dawn. I dialoged with the Lord, asking hard questions and giving Him all my concerns.

"A time to give birth and a time to die;
a time to plant and a time to uproot what is planted."
— Ecclesiastes 3:2

The sun began to rise from the east. The sky turned from a dark gray to a lighter grayish blue with a tinge of tangerine and pink. The stars twinkled with an extra surge before giving way to the sun's performance for the day. The trees, silhouettes of grace, displayed their colors. Leaves crackled beneath my feet.

I was suddenly aware that I wasn't alone. I was being followed, guided, and surrounded.

"A time to weep and a time to laugh;
a time to mourn and a time to dance."
— Ecclesiastes 3:4

They glided with direction, yet with a carefree air about them. They floated with purpose, yet somehow relaxation.

Butterflies... Large, yellow and black, magnificent... They were tiger swallowtail butterflies.

With the sun's first beams and the fading of the pathway lights, the butterflies flew from their resting spot on tree limbs to exercise their wings, to play in the dapple of the shadows, and to gift me with amazing grace. They flew ahead of me, behind me, over me, and with me. Every morning I arose anxious to walk, pray, and delight in this gift God orchestrated for me. The butterflies never slept in, never failed to meet me in my sunrise strolls. My cocoon of grief transformed before me, releasing the Holy Spirit's comfort on the wings of butterflies. I knew His great love for me through them. I knew His care for my broken heart, and I knew heaven on earth.

"He has made everything appropriate in its time.
He has also set eternity in their heart..."
— Ecclesiastes 3:11

Throughout that summer, and still to this day as I write this, the butterflies became ministers to me, affirming God's answer for the comfort my soul so desperately needed. When they fluttered, I saw promises painted on their wings. They stirred me on to worship and exalt God. I was once crawling on my belly in my own sin, separated from God. Yet, He purposed for me, for all of us, to be beautiful in His sight. He transformed me for His glory, and He would do the same for anyone that was willing. He declared me His beloved, a woman who had lost a son from sickness and pain. God made peace in my heart when I chose to submit to His eternal plan.

The butterfly miraculously goes through a metamorphosis, growing his wings while hunkered down and humbled, waiting and believing in something better. His hope arises in the morning light. If they hid in the trees and we found them dead on the ground, how would we know about their beauty in pure flight, the way they dance through the wildflowers and the gardens of life?

Eternity spread its wings in my heart, and I was purposed to fly, grateful for the hope that carried me on butterfly breezes of His Holy Spirit. A certain verse became so alive to me. I didn't always understand His will, but I knew His will was good.

"And do not be conformed to this world, but be transformed by the renewing of your mind, so that you may prove what the will of God is, that which is good and acceptable and perfect."
— Romans 12:2

I knew Tim was now living in perfection in heaven…because God was, and would always remain, good.

My grief did not fly away, but I felt the fluttering of the Holy Spirit so strongly within. I knew His love and peace; I knew that the prayers of many were holding me together. While turbulence was expected, I also knew in my heart that He would provide a safe landing with many lights along the runway.

P.S. I wouldn't put this together until several months into writing this, but the name of the hospital Timmy passed away in was "Park View."

PLAYLIST IX

It Is Well

1. "Free" — Switchfoot
2. "Use Somebody" — Kings of Leon
3. "Taken at All" — Crosby, Stills & Nash
4. "War of My Life" — John Mayer
5. "Be Yourself" — Graham Nash
6. "Revelation" — Third Day
7. "Never Be the Same" — Red
8. "From the Inside Out" — Seventh Day Slumber
9. "Bring the Rain" — MercyMe
10. "Open Hands" — Matt Papa
11. "I'm Yours" — Jason Mraz
12. "How You Live (Turn Up the Music)" — Point of Grace
13. "Everything Glorious" — David Crowder Band
14. "I Will Rise" — Chris Tomlin
15. "In Christ Alone" — Matt Papa
16. "How He Loves" — David Crowder Band
17. "Beautiful Ending" — BarlowGirl

Chapter 21

To Heal and to Help

The days moved swiftly. In the year prior, I re-involved myself with church and the sheep by attending a small group. Strong leadership helped me connect to people and trust a core group of friends. I'd become so consumed with all of our moving, keeping my children healthy, and various other life struggles that I had slowly slipped into the margins of church life for several years. A few special ladies pulled me back into their graces, covering my family in prayer and accountability. I gathered at Starbucks with them on Tuesday evenings.

God began a rough draft of His own, and He didn't need an editor for any of His manuscripts. Within my small group, a powerful story was locked away, its author purposefully avoiding any spotlight or discovery of her hidden talent.

Knowing the depths of despair herself, how could God possibly reignite a fire in her for writing and editing she thought she buried in all her trials?

I hardly knew this woman, but God brought us together through a mutual friend. A vision soon began to form from the desire to heal and help.

~~~

One Saturday I read an article in my local paper about a

"Million Mom March." A local woman wanted to raise awareness for mothers who were suffering the loss of their children as a result of street gangs and violence. The woman was not only broken by the loss of her adult son, but her heart also hurt for her community.

I decided to go to the march. The walk left Ganesha Park in Pomona and wound down to the community center through a few rough neighborhoods and business districts. Families carried signs and sang hymns as we marched.

Once we arrived at the community center, a few speeches were given and then we gathered in a circle, holding hands as we united in prayer, asking for healing, protection, and God's grace. I received a shirt and a lot of hugs from new friends. I heard stories of heartache and shared a little myself. I normally wouldn't have crossed paths with any of these women, but the Lord brought me out of my own bubble and connected me to a greater community. It helped me. It helped others.

~~~

A Million Moms

(Inspired by the Million Mom March, August 18, 2007)

Can there be a million moms
Who cry for their departed children?
They raise their hands to God,
"Oh, why this special burden?"

A million moms there are,

And a million grieved dads too.
Our tears flood the rivers
Flowing from our hearts, broken through.

Our children went before us,
So a part of us is gone.
But the Holy Spirit's voice
Shows us how to move on.

"Move on," You say. But how
Can I ever be the same?
My baby's voice is gone,
My heart echoes his name.

"I am a God of compassion,
And comfort to you I will send.
You will have a new purpose,
Your message, to help hearts mend.

I know the number of your tears
And hear your prayers' lament.
Glorified in heaven now,
Your child's life, a new fulfillment.

So tell your story of courage,
Your dreams for them you had.
I have given you a new vision.
In heaven, your children are glad."

Yes, you'll always miss them.
Understand they're now perfect up there.
To watch over us here on earth,
As you move on and show others you care.

May your burden become one of great joy,
A peace only God can bring.
A million souls touched by God,
Until reunited, our hope we will sing!

~~~

Journaling, like food, kept me nourished, but I also needed a snack and maybe even some dessert. A Christ-based website called FaithWriters provided a sweet treat. I enjoyed the work of the imagination, putting sentences together and telling stories. The weekly challenges from FaithWriters focused my mind on things other than my grief. I became actively involved and started to make cyber writing pals who encouraged me. I also started sharing little tidbits of my work with close friends. For the first time, my writing started to go beyond my own journals. It was scary to put myself out there... Who likes criticism, anyway?

"...he who listens to reproof acquires understanding."
— Proverbs 15:32

Sometimes I wrote little devotions and shared them with my small group. I used that insight to further make connections with every day, mundane things and God's Word. I had to keep writing, putting into action what my grief counselor told me to do. I had the choice to make it either a blessing or a curse. I chose to make it a blessing!

I also developed a family "newsletter" which taught me more of the ins and outs of using a computer to manipulate pictures and formatting. These newsletters were a test to see how writing for others would go. It also gave me an opportunity to share my thoughts and how God's attention to my grief manifested itself. I wanted those "butterfly feelings," that pathway I walked along, to connect to the work of the Holy Spirit.

I really didn't know what God had planned for my life, but I liked where I was headed. Writing gave me a sense of peace and sharing what I wrote gave me purpose.

"Trust in the Lord with all your heart
and do not lean on your own understanding.
In all your ways acknowledge Him,
and He will make your paths straight."
— Proverbs 3:5-6

PLAYLIST X

Keep On Singing

1. "The Blues" — Switchfoot
2. "Changes" — 3 Doors Down
3. "When I'm Gone" — 3 Doors Down
4. "Quasimodo" — Lifehouse
5. "Jesus, Take the Wheel" — Carrie Underwood
6. "Never Too Late" — Three Days Grace
7. "Vertigo" — U2
8. "Lucky" — Hoobastank
9. "Keep on Singin' My Song" — Christina Aguilera
10. "Letting Go" — Jeremy Camp
11. "Angel" — Sarah McLachlan
12. "On Jordan's Stormy Banks I Stand" — Jars of Clay
13. "All My Tears" — Jars of Clay
14. "All My Praise" — Selah
15. "Yesterdays" — Switchfoot
16. "What Hurts the Most" — Rascal Flatts
17. "When You Are Near" — Jeremy Camp

Chapter 22

In the "Grand" Stands

"The thrill of victory…the agony of defeat…"

Tim debated that topic on any given sport, even curling. During Winter Olympic years, you'd find him watching games on ESPN 3 at 3:00 in the morning. Intense and passionate, he filled himself with the knowledge of every single sport out there, as well as the details of strategy and statistics, the media, and commentary shows. He was a super fan in every sense of the word. I missed his presence in the living room, cheering for a team, flipping through channels, and making NCAA brackets.

Now, I needed to remind myself, Tim had inherited box seats for every sports venue in the universe.

In 2000, my 20-year-old son told me about a basketball superstar who played for the Miami Heat. His name was Alonzo Mourning and he was diagnosed with focal segmental glomerulosclerosis—the same kidney disease Tim had. The condition required Mourning to have a transplant. We followed his comeback and career ever since. Tim tried to write him, but we never received a correspondence back. Alonzo Mourning went on to win an NBA Championship in 2006.

In August 2007, the "boys of summer" played baseball in "Field of Dreams." A certain major leaguer continued to smack the ball out and beyond, approaching a record-breaking moment in history. His name was Barry Bonds. Every time he stepped into the batter's box, the announcers and fans began speculating. He was a very controversial player, just the kind Tim loved to chatter about.

When Barry Bonds hit that ball and broke Hank Aaron's record, I needed the dialogue… I needed the commentary, so I wrote.

~~~

Number 756

Hey Son, can you see from up there?
Barry Bonds broke Hank's record you know.
That baseball did soar
Through the air, here below.

It came in the 5th,
With one out, ball pitched.
Like him or not;
Truth or just myth.

Number 756
Hit at 84 miles per hour.
Did he cheat?
Will this legacy taste sour?

I remember Tim,
your fast-talking chatter
About all things sports,
Even Barry Bonds, this great batter.

But in heaven I am sure
It is not homeruns that count,
But how many times
You've prayed about your doubt.

Can we count our prayers
As they soar to God's ears?
Would one break a record
Of saintly amens in a career?

I do not think God keeps
A statistic like this.
Every prayer to Him is
A homerun on His list.

Maybe this is your job, Son,
A record of prayerful fans,
Awarded in heaven's Hall of Fame,
All a part of the Master's plan.

~~~

"Do you not know that those who run in a race all run,
but only one receives the prize?
Run in such a way that you may win."
— 1 Corinthians 9:24

Some days I ran out of breath. The Lord became my personal trainer. I knew I had to continue to gain strength for my family and for myself. I needed to live out my life in God's game plan.

One day I left to go to work and I saw the strangest sight. A very tall, awkward looking man made his way down my street...jogging backward. He occasionally looked over his shoulder, but he seemed very confident in what he was doing. I thought all day about that strange sight.

When I got home, I looked it up on the web, curious as to what the benefits were for such an exercise. Six bullet points filled the page about how running backward was beneficial...

- *Post-surgical rehab*

- *Moving backward might take the pressure off certain muscle strains*

- *Lower-extremity injuries*

- *When you've tried drugs, ice/heat, physical therapy, stretching, and strength training with no results*

- *For those looking for a different stimulus or cross-training*

- *Benefits those who may need to change directions rapidly and/or run backward in his or her sport*

I wondered if jogging backward—emotionally, that is— would be something to make me stronger, not sadder. In my case, maybe looking back at hard memories would be a sort of workout for my aching heart. I needed to move through my grief into Spirit-filled rehabilitation and there was no better coach than the Lord. Memories took the pressure off my hurting heart and stimulated my feet to move forward, calming my stomach. Face exercises lifted my countenance.

The world offered its numbing substitutes, but I knew they were empty promises. The Lord offered me hope, peace, and purpose. I was quite the klutz when it came to athletic activities, but I could not let my grief bench me any longer. I needed to stay on track, keep trusting my coach, fix my eyes on above, and focus on the prize. These were the benefits of my continued spiritual workout in the rehabilitation of my broken heart.

I never saw the guy running backward again. Reflecting angelic qualities, I watched him disappear into the gloom of the June morning.

"Therefore, since we have so great a cloud of witnesses surrounding us, let us also lay aside every encumbrance and the sin which so easily entangles us, and let us run with endurance the race that is set before us, fixing our eyes on Jesus, the author and perfecter of faith…"
— Hebrews 12:1-2

When you know the Lord, death won't defeat you. In the dugout of the body of Christ, I continued to move toward my own victory, one inning at a time. Tim, my rally monkey, had already crossed home plate and God's team reigned victorious.

PLAYLIST XI

Peace

1. "One Tribe" — Black Eyed Peas
2. "Words" — Train
3. "The Reason for The World" — Matthew West
4. "Times" — Tenth Avenue North
5. "I'm Still Yours" — Kutless
6. "Parachute" — Train
7. "Something Beautiful" — NEEDTOBREATHE
8. "The Finish Line" — Train
9. "The Shape of You" — Jewel
10. "Alive Again" — Matt Maher
11. "Help Is On the Way" — Michael W. Smith
12. "Don't Wait" — Addison Road
13. "Blessings" — Laura Story
14. "Beautiful" — MercyMe
15. "What Faith Can Do" — Kutless
16. "You Are Loved (Don't Give Up)" — Josh Groban

Chapter 23

"Happy Birthday Timmy!"

"So teach us to number our days,
that we may present to You a heart of wisdom."
— Psalm 90:12

The calendar flipped and September arrived, and with it another point of focused grief. Tim's birthday was circled on the calendar—September 25. After securing a few days off of work, we decided to go somewhere and celebrate with a family outing, just Ted, Corey, and me.

We drove down to Long Beach and visited the Aquarium of the Pacific. Instead of eating out, we enjoyed the evening eating tacos with our friends, the Lollis family. They were the same people who blessed us with a meal the previous Mother's Day. We survived the day by being together as a family, being proactive, intentional, and thankful for the opportunity to celebrate still. I felt Tim smiling down at us, taking a break from his own heavenly party. When we returned home in the very warm evening, candles began to appear.

A power outage darkened the neighborhood. It was a sultry, Indian summer evening; we moved outdoors with our neighbors and started sharing sodas, conversation, and flashlights. Tim always loved and craved attention. I smiled to myself thinking that he had something to do with this, "creating" this outdoor gathering in our new Chino home.

With candles and flashlights aglow, light shined despite a certain spark dimmed.

I felt the love of God in a powerful way that night. We made wishes, prayed with thankful hearts, and were doused with a heavenly comfort. God's amazing grace opened up to a full reward, even on the most bittersweet day.

As the years went by, we decided to celebrate Tim's birthday as though it was a national holiday; we called them "Timmy Days" or "Timmy Weekends," depending on the calendar and our budget. Every trip we have taken to honor Tim has been perfect in beauty, inspiration, and fun. We know Tim is always with us in spirit on those days.

We usually go out to dinner at a nice restaurant on the evening of his birthday, asking the hostess to escort us to a table that is set for four—our "missing man" formation, I like to call it. When we are asked, I end up sharing that "We're celebrating my son's birthday who is heaven." I'm sure that's not a very common answer, judging by the reactions we get. Usually, our servers will prod and question a bit deeper. More often than not, they've shared a grief story of their own and were encouraged by the way we "celebrate" a hard family occasion. Each year, I believe that God goes before us and prepares the hearts of those we will cross paths with.

"Make us glad according to the days You have afflicted us,
and the years we have seen evil.
Let Your work appear to Your servants
and Your majesty to their children.

Let the favor of the Lord our God be upon us;
and confirm for us the work of our hands;
yes, confirm the work of our hands."
— Psalm 90:15-17

~~~

A Heavenly Birthday
(from Tim)

A heavenly host of angels
Sing a Happy Birthday song
All in tune and harmony;
This is where I belong.

In heaven for eternity,
Praising God with no more pain.
His great love saved me,
An Amazing Grace gain.

A perfect body and spirit,
What a great present to receive.
On streets of gold I run and play,
It's Home where I can breathe.

Let's celebrate the Light;
Raise a candle in the air.
My darkness is gone forever,
Heavenly birthdays can't compare.

Timmy Days

- 2007 — Aquarium of the Pacific; Dinner at the Lollis' House
- 2008 — SeaWorld San Diego; Hunter Restaurant
- 2009 — San Diego Zoo; Casa Guadalajara; Old Town San Diego
- 2010 — San Francisco; Hard Rock Café; Fisherman's Wharf
- 2011 — Downtown Disney; House of Blues
- 2012 — Carlsbad, CA; Chart House
- 2013 — Ronald Reagan Presidential Library; Ventura Harbor; Aloha Steakhouse
- 2014 — Friday night Dodger's game; Dodger Dogs and cold beer; a trip to Solvang and the Santa Barbara coast
- 2015 — Central Coast; Cambria and Hearst Castle; Cambria Pub and Steakhouse
- 2016 — Palm Desert; Joshua Tree National Park; Outback Steakhouse
- 2017 — Lake Arrowhead; Catalina Island; Bluewater Avalon
- 2018 — Dana Point Harbor; whale watching; San Juan Capistrano Mission; Harbor Grill Restaurant
- 2019 — Chino High School Homecoming football game; Spunky Steer; Oak Glen day trip

PLAYLIST XII

Change

1. "Away from the Sun" — 3 Doors Down
2. "The Least That You Could Do" — Inside The Outside
3. "Better That We Break" — Maroon 5
4. "You Can Close Your Eyes" — Sheryl Crow
5. "Chasing Cars" — Snow Patrol
6. "Yahweh" — U2
7. "Perfect Girl" — Sarah McLachlan
8. "Feels Like" — Jeremy Camp
9. "Fix You" — Coldplay
10. "Have You Ever Seen the Rain" — Creedence Clearwater Revival
11. "These Hard Times" — Matchbox Twenty
12. "I Lift My Eyes Up" — Kutless
13. "How Far We've Come" — Matchbox Twenty
14. "Do Something" — Eagles
15. "Fields of Grace" — Big Daddy Weave
16. "The Change Inside of Me" — MercyMe
17. "Fall Down" — MercyMe

Chapter 24

Changing Seasons

The stubborn California summer dug in until around September. However, fall eventually showed up on the scene, kicked summer out of the bed, and pulled up the covers. We didn't feel the weather change until around late October that year. By then, the school year had already started and my job as a one-on-one aide in special education kept me busy. My student that year was a senior and needed a lot of attention.

As we got settled in our new home, we realized how different it felt. After being uprooted for four years, I didn't feel comfortable anywhere. I felt anxious and restless. I asked God for His security in my life.

Can we settle here, Lord? Can I know what a home is again?

The yard at the new house needed plenty of attention. Fortunately, I loved to garden. There was only one overgrown orange tree that provided any shade or color. Dirt completely surrounded the house. I kept myself busy landscaping. Like painting, I viewed gardening as a blank canvas; I had a lot of ideas to bring our yard to life. I began seeding, planting, and preparing for both visual pleasure and physical sustenance. While I waited for the dead lawn to revive, a pumpkin seed fell deep into the earth.

It grew. Across the sparse grass, it stretched, flowered, and developed fruit.

Around that same time, I decided to write another family newsletter. As long and full as the pumpkin vine grew, it only produced two pumpkins. To me, that was perfect—one in memory of Tim and one for Corey. The following poem highlighted my fall newsletter.

~~~

Pumpkin Patch

From a seed grows a sprout
Out of a hard outer shell.
Tender and vulnerable,
The shoot starts to swell.

A couple of green leaves
Unfold and stretch out.
A yellow flower appears
As the bees buzz about.

Last summer's heat,
Like a furnace it burned
Warming the night air,
Bringing garden concern.

Keep the soil moist
And the pests at bay.
Green pumpkins are growing,
Getting bigger each day.

So fun to watch
To check on each morn.
I remember the first day
The budded fruit formed.

As God cares for us,
We can give Him the same honor;
Whether new believers or
seasoned warriors.

For He is our Father,
He plants us for light
To bear fruit in the harvest,
Share His love, eternal life.

Adding spice and pure sweetness
When we take the time to tend
To our hard outer shell,
Our inner core He mends.

So enjoy the harvest time,
All the smiling pumpkin faces.
Let God's light shine through
In all your everyday places.

~~~

I was reminded that the pumpkin, an icon of the fall season, served us in so many capacities—pie, bread, jack-o-lanterns, roasted seeds, scarecrow heads, décor, and pumpkin spice lattes! Yet, they only grew in a specific season. God gifted me with the symbol of the Holy Spirit in the butterfly, and now I embraced the pumpkin as a reminder of seeds of love and a light that continues to shine in the dark. More and more, I observed the things of nature. When I took the time to listen to His still, quiet voice, God in all His glory was recognizable in every aspect of life.

"For since the creation of the world His invisible attributes, His eternal power and divine nature, have been clearly seen, being understood through what has been made, so that they are without excuse."
— Romans 1:20

~~~

Ted's best friend since high school, Angel, enlisted in the army to train as a nurse. Meanwhile, Ted stayed behind to work in the home-building trade. They had played football, attended "Youth for Christ" activities, partied, camped, hiked, and survived crazy, youthful antics together. Angel was also the best man at our wedding. Their bond, one that always picked up right where they left off, stayed intact throughout Angel's military service.

Eventually, Angel decided to make a career out of the U.S. Army. He met his bride, Dianne, while serving our country as a nurse. They settled together on the East Coast and Angel deployed as an evac-nurse. Dianne resumed her nursing duties with the Department of Veterans Affairs stateside. They went on to become the parents of two boys, yet another commonality we shared.

On October 28, 2007, Ted returned home from dropping Corey off somewhere. He walked in the door, visibly upset and shaking with sadness. I did that frequently, but Ted didn't; he usually held back his emotions with gut-busting strength.

What was going on?

While Ted was driving, he'd received a phone call. He relayed to me the terrible news. Angel and Dianne's oldest son had fallen and sustained a terrible head injury. He was an adult, moved out of his parents' house, and, assuming adult responsibilities, he didn't think the injury required medical attention. He went to bed later that night and never woke up. He passed away exactly eight months from the day of Tim's passing.

Angel, who had been serving in Iraq and Afghanistan at the time, triaging the mortally wounded, and Dianne, who had been tending to the shrapnel-filled, limbless soldiers, now had a tragedy to face at home.

Heart needs restarting, blood needs transfusing, and immediate transport off the battlefield is required. Wrap gauze all around the soul... Wait! They can't breathe! We need resuscitation!

Ted and I bled out for our dear friends who grieved over their firstborn son on the other side of the country. Our sewn-up injuries were reopened and began to fester. Once again, we came to the cross to receive healing, to pray for peace, and to intercede on behalf of our friends who were in desperate need of intensive care from the Lord.

"Surely our griefs He Himself bore,
and our sorrows He carried;

yet we ourselves esteemed Him stricken,
smitten of God, and afflicted.
But He was pierced through for our transgressions,
He was crushed for our iniquities…"
— Isaiah 53:4-5

~~~

We picked the pumpkins; they sat out on our front porch steps. I visited the grocery store and viewed gourds in various colors and shapes. The white pumpkins shined bright, contrasting with the orange and gold ones. I bought two and set them with our homegrown orange ones. The next day was November 1—the month of Thanksgiving. It was a month to thank the Lord for all He gave us and a month to trust in His plan.

Chapter 25

Kingdom of Our Hearts

"For behold, the kingdom of God is in your midst."
— Luke 17:21

November came and I shuddered—not so much from the cooler air, but from the sadness that seemed to rain upon me. I lost my father to cancer a week before Thanksgiving in 1982 and my mother on Thanksgiving Day in 2000. Then, in 2003, our home sizzled like a turkey in a deep fryer two days before Thanksgiving.

This year, 2007, my mother's best friend since junior high called me on November 20. I knew the occasion, as Judy and I had spoken earlier that same week. Her sweet daughter, my own childhood friend, Carrie, succumbed to her battle with metastatic breast cancer.

I had heard a sermon the previous week on the Beatitudes.

"Blessed are those who mourn,
for they shall be comforted."
— Matthew 5:4

I needed that verse. I needed to believe in that verse. I needed to give that verse time to play out in my life.

I knew the stealer of my joy loved to remind me of my failures, regrets, disappointments, and hurts. I knew the devil wanted me to stay in that frame of mind so I wouldn't remember the victory that God had completed on the cross.

November marked a time of harvest and comfort food, blessings and gratitude. Despite my loss, I knew that God had put a beautiful place setting down for me at His table. He wrote me a name card in gold script by His own hand. He prepared a menu of grace upon grace that simmered in His purpose. My son, Tim, had arrived early for the feast. The fullness of God, prepared in love, came basted in hope and was served faithfully when I came to His table of mercy. I was determined, this November, to find a new recipe for my soul and allow God to supply all the ingredients I needed.

Watching football on TV all day wouldn't work. Stuffing ourselves wouldn't cut it. We didn't need fancy silverware or pie. What we needed was a happy place...*the* happiest place, actually.

I had a student whose father was employed at Disneyland. He offered us entrance to the park and signed us in at the opening turnstile when we got to the Magic Kingdom. It was a perfect fall day. Our plates were filled with adventure, fantasy, storytelling, and laughter.

At about 4:00 PM, the sun began its slow descent and we got in line for Splash Mountain. We knew there was a possibility of getting a bit wet as the ride careened down the mountain, but we took the risk. Corey, a large young man, and several other bulky people sat in front of Ted and me. When we got to the bottom, we were more than wet; we were completely soaked through. Water was even pooling inside my tennis shoes. As the sun found the horizon, we shivered and laughed about our predicament.

We only lived about 40 minutes away from Anaheim, so we returned home, changed our clothes, and got back to the park by 6:00 PM for our Thanksgiving dinner.

God hung out with us that day at Disneyland. The park was decorated for Christmas and each ride reminded us that another holiday loomed around the corner, just a few short weeks away. While we floated through the Haunted Mansion ride, I saw a big, decorated Christmas tree. Presents were stacked under it. I looked closer.

For a moment, time seemed to stand still. One huge gift, stacked neatly beneath the tree, faced me. It was tagged with a name—*Timmy B.*

We left the park at midnight, exhausted and delighted that we were able to make a new memory this Thanksgiving. Snow, like marshmallows, covered the castle and our hearts were full. Though grief is not gravy, God continued to give me extra helpings of His grace and mercy, showing me that His bounty was complete, and I could rest in the fullness of His love. His tenderness triumphed and His sweetness satisfied like pie à la mode. I was reminded that I could always go back to Him, even in the middle of my darkest nights, and He would refresh me. He would never run out of goodness.

"O give thanks to the Lord for He is good;
for His lovingkindness is everlasting."
— 1 Chronicles 16:34

~~~

Thanksgiving at the Magic Kingdom

"The Happiest Place on Earth,"
Everyone wants to go there.
At any time you can venture;
Rest your heart from all your cares.

At the Park, off to discover
Snow on the castle and a Christmas tree divine.
Disney magic is working;
We feel good inside, thankful and fine.

The Matterhorn and Nemo,
Poinsettias and Pluto,
Thunder Mountain Railroad,
And pirates like Jack Sparrow.

And then there is "Splash Mountain,"
Brer Rabbit and Brer Fox reside.
But that splash…a drench.
A dunk of a ride.

Dry again, back to the Park
After our mountain deluge
For a "first" Thanksgiving meal,
A dinner refuge.

Sat at a table with four chairs;
Brought to a moment and a tear.
Bowed our head in remembrance
Of one no longer with us this year.

But along in the spirit, I know you were there
For you "appeared" in the mansion for me.
Your name "Timmy B." in big letters stood out
On a gift tag under the tree.

We can make a magical day again,
Find Thanksgiving in heavenly courts.
For God is the Maker of Happiness,
Placed deep in the Kingdom of our hearts.

Chapter 26

A Season with Reason

I received news at the beginning of December that an essay I entered into a contest a few months prior had won first place! Somehow, within my grief-struggling days, I came across this local contest, wrote a story, and submitted it on a whim. When I got the news it won, I believed it to be affirmation from above. That little accolade gave me a sense that my writing just might be something worth sharing.

I started writing relentlessly, almost obsessively. It was truly the only thing I wanted to do. The Christmas decorations stayed in their boxes that year, and I didn't set up a tree. Yet, God placed two decorating, designer elves—my friend, Becky, and her daughter, Courtney—in my living room on Wednesday evening after I'd left for church.

When I came home later that evening, I saw my bannister wrapped in beautiful greenery, red and gold velvet bows, and lights that were twinkling as though they were announcing a stairway to heaven. One of our end tables was adorned with a poem about a loved one's first Christmas spent in heaven. Two tiny Christmas trees, one for each of my sons, balanced at the ends. There was a wooden sleigh underneath the first tree and a crystal angel next to the other. Next to it all sat my mother's Bible.

Unbeknownst to me, Becky had also sent one of my poems about Tim to the management at Disneyland. As a thank you, they sent a box filled with t-shirts and Disney holiday décor, bringing cheer to our home and our new memories to the forefront of our minds.

"Joy to the world," the carolers sang.

Could joy possibly find its way through the hall of melancholy?

I looked over at the sleigh, a wooden cutout that was glued together in a Cub Scout meeting by Timmy. A picture of him in his uniform was stuck to the front, framed in red matting.

Traditionally, our Christmas decorations were stored every year in plastic bins in the garage, resting until after Thanksgiving. However, the fire that overtook our home in 2003 burned everything up. I was only able to salvage a few things… Timmy's sleigh was one of them. It was singed on one side, symbolizing its survival among the ashes. I usually decorated the house in abundance. Now, simple seemed more appropriate.

I opened up to Psalm 23 in my mother's Bible; it was a tangible, yet spiritual prayer about seeking after God and His will.

The story I sent to be published in WestCoast Magazine was called, "The Most Meaningful Gift I Ever Received." It told the story of how I taught my boys to wrap presents and how that coincided with the unwrapping of God's gift of amazing grace. I saw His amazing grace in a song sung by my son in a hospital bed as much as I did at the sight of baby

Jesus in a manger. Through tears, I focused on the reason for the season. Then, I sat down and penned my annual Christmas poem.

~~~

This Christmas

This Christmas, I want the Season to be,
All about you God and nothing about me.
Christmases past, a blessing for sure,
But this Christmas is different; its meaning more pure.

This Christmas, with every chorus I sing,
Praises to you God, sweeter I bring.
For I want You glorified, Your peace I do have
Though great heartache walked onto my path.

This Christmas, Jesus, Your name rejoice
For I know my son's in heaven, with a new singing voice.
No longer in pain, but looking down from above.
The loneliness gives way to God's awesome love.

This Christmas, God, thank You for eternal life,
Forgiveness of sin through Christ's pain and strife...
For gifts of gold in family and friends;
Your Word and Spirit, broken hearts can mend.

This Christmas, my prayer for you as well,
To search your heart and see if in it does dwell,
The Babe in a manger whose message of peace,
Starts within your heart, His love increased.

This Christmas, my focus on not what is external,
But in Christ, God's greatest gift, eternal.
Know that I wish the same for you and yours;
He is the Reason for the Season, for you He truly adores.

*"And the Word became flesh, and dwelt among us, and we
saw His glory, glory as of the only begotten from the
Father, full of grace and truth."*
— John 1:14

Merry Christmas, 2007

~~~

As the days drew nearer to December 25, my restlessness ramped up. I kept Christmas music on, but my mixer and cookie recipes stayed hidden in the cupboard. One night, when meeting with my small group, I did a crazy thing and volunteered to host our Christmas dinner and ornament exchange party at my house. I figured that keeping busy would help; it would just be one more thing to get me through the few days left of the holiday season.

As I planned the event, I decided that I'd share something inspirational from a book with the group. With my thoughts consumed on heaven, Christmas, and angels, I searched through unpacked boxes for a book written by Billy Graham called, *Angels*.

I found it and opened the dusty cover. As if sent from heaven itself, a note floated to the floor at my feet. I bent down, retrieved it, and read the words that were reserved for such a time as this. An overwhelmingly spiritual encounter with the Holy Spirit prompted me to join the small group, and now a divine encounter from the Comforter of the Christmas season struck me. I sat stunned, filled with love and basking in the palpable presence of the Holy Spirit. I wept with pure, amazing joy as I read the words in an all-too-familiar handwriting...

"Tears are a way to meet a heart frozen in grief."

It belonged to my own mother, who passed away seven years prior. At 49 years old, she lost my father to cancer. She found love again, only to lose him to cancer as well. Mike, the owner of Crown Pacific Properties, came to be a significant part of our family. He and my mother found a deep friendship and compatibility. Together, they grew in strength and a deeper understanding of the Lord. When my mother lost Mike, she found herself in a season of intense grief. It wasn't until later on that she discovered the beauty of grace in her life.

Now, she bent down from heaven to me. With the guidance of the Holy Spirit, this note came to me just three days out from Christmas. God wanted me to know that our holiday party was not about angels, but about heaven, family, and the winter season. It was a holiday that deserved to be celebrated even though I felt frozen in the past. God's plan to guide me through the season was astoundingly clear. I had an acute awareness of His continual presence and mercy in my life. He took my own frozen heart and gently warmed it up with precious love from my own mother. He gave me the thought to find a dusty old book and the miracle of Christmas came shining into my dining room because of it.

The Messiah had come… Hallelujah and glory to God in the highest! I had a Redeemer whose name was Immanuel! He was with me!

Tim and his grandma were not missing one moment of this Christmas celebration. My heart began to thaw. Tears of humble adoration for what He brought to me that lonely winter afternoon fell down my cheeks; they felt like healing, like a warm blanket or a roaring fireplace.

God's grace was extended to the whole world, which He so loved, when He sent His son to earth in the form of a perfect baby who had been born of a virgin. That child grew up to be a man who faithfully obeyed His Father, even to the point of death on a cross. He reconciled man to God through His crucifixion.

"By this the love of God was manifested in us, that God has sent His only begotten Son into the world so that we might live through Him.
In this is love, not that we loved God, but that He loved us and sent His Son to be the propitiation for our sins."
— 1 John 4:9-10

With the new year right around the corner, I knew that days would roll into days and each sunrise brought with it a memory. Most days were incredibly hard, but there were good days in which His presence in my life overwhelmed me and filled me with comfort. I knew the Lord had more of those types of days planned for me. This was the hope I found—to anticipate a whisper, a note, a verse, a song, a butterfly, or whatever God had for me at any time throughout the day. Those days, like a fully charged battery, surged me forward with a confidence that the Lord would minister to me personally and paid close attention to the needs of my heart.

There were some things that I understood so perfectly and obviously; other things remained a mystery. I knew a specific path was set before me and I needed to stay on it. I needed to keep my eyes on Him and my heart open. As I pressed into Him daily and waited in anticipation, I found comfort and more of my purpose. I continued to journal, using my written words to speak to God.

Yes, my grief journey would be long, but rest stops that provided healing came frequently and the Lord continued to lead me into more and more days of amazing grace.

PLAYLIST XIII

2007 Christmas Memorial Mix

1. "In The Bleak Midwinter" — Jars of Clay
2. "Angels Among Us" — Alabama
3. "Mary, Did You Know" — Natalie Cole
4. "Breath of Heaven (Mary's Song)" — Amy Grant
5. "Silent Night" — Josh Groban
6. "The Miracle of Christmas" — Steven Curtis Chapman
7. "My Christmas Prayer" — Bebe Winans (feat. Rob Thomas)
8. "Angels We Have Heard on High/Joy to the World" — Michael Crawford
9. "Sleep Well" — Todd Agnew (feat. Shelley Jennings)
10. "When The River Meets the Sea" — John Denver (feat. The Muppets)
11. "I Heard the Bells On Christmas Day" — MercyMe
12. "God with Us" — Todd Agnew
13. "Angels from The Realms of Glory" — Steven Curtis Chapman
14. "Thankful" — Josh Groban

A Philippian Proverb

Rejoice in the Lord always; again I will say, rejoice!

TRUST IN THE LORD WITH ALL YOUR HEART

Let your gentle spirit be known to all men. The Lord is near.

AND DO NOT LEAN ON YOUR OWN UNDERSTANDING

Be anxious for nothing, but in everything by prayer and supplication with thanksgiving let your requests be made known to God.

IN ALL YOUR WAYS ACKNOWLEDGE HIM

And the peace of God, which surpasses all comprehension, will guard your hearts and your minds in Christ Jesus.

AND HE WILL MAKE YOUR PATHS STRAIGHT

— Philippians 4:4-7
— Proverbs 3:5-6

Chapter 27

Renewed Passion and a Continued Hope

Christmas passed and the new year made its bittersweet appearance. We mustered through every Christmas song, bearing a deeper meaning from them. A stocking hung from the mantle with a heavy heart. Tim's time on earth ended in late February of 2007, meaning we'd endured the earth without him for 10 months. I closed my eyes and could still feel him, smell him, and hear him. I asked the Lord how long those feelings would be with me.

I fine-tuned the lyrics of Christmas songs in my heart. I no longer found purpose in these songs for just the Christmas season, but for the rest of my seasons.

Be near me, Lord Jesus, I ask Thee to stay
Close by me forever, and love me I pray
Bless all the dear children, in Thy tender care
And fit us for heaven, to live with Thee there

Friends remembered us and we felt their love. Tim's buddies called, heartfelt words were penned in cards, and we received many invitations for social gatherings.

That year, our church put on a production called, "The Journey." In addition to the musical, a display of writing, artwork, crafting, and needlework submitted by various members of our congregation was displayed in the narthex. I decided to participate by adding a few drawings I'd worked on over the previous summer. It felt good to draw again. There was a certain sense of satisfaction in the feeling of finishing a project and seeing it framed. My spirits were lifted by it. I was even commissioned by a friend to recreate a favorite picture of hers after she saw my art.

I chose pastels, gathered my crayons, and began working. God was resurrecting a lost art within me; it was always something I enjoyed but felt insecure in. My ability to see beyond the obvious kept me looking for God in everything. He became very present, even in the mundane. I felt a surge of confidence at the discovery of a dormant passion, as well as in my writing. I sketched out a few ideas and illustrations, stimulating the forgotten artist buried within me.

I kept myself intentionally busy. I involved myself with many different groups and social events, and Ted started attending church more regularly. I knew the prayers from those close to us kept us protected and healthy, both mentally and spiritually. My Sunday school class captivated my soul every week with excellent teaching and fellowship. I submitted things regularly to the FaithWriters website and my writing began to improve. I felt a true passion for words and creating stories. Several of my submissions were placed in the "Top Three" category.

Thank you, Lord, for giving me one more thing to keep my mind busy with. Do not let this turn into a form of crazy obsession. Keep me focused, Lord, not weary. Amen.

I submitted consistently and received constructive

critiques, which was a definite form of grace. I also made new friends across the country that loved to write and loved the Lord. What a blessing!

~~~

The news broke and my heart took another hit. It wasn't anybody I knew personally; I just knew *of* him, but it devastated me all the same. I wrote two whole pages about my feelings; the page was marked with the date—January 22, 2008. Heath Ledger, the young, up-and-coming actor was found dead from an apparent overdose at the age of 28.

People Magazine described him as "an intense, restless man known as much for his partying and wild streak as his sweetness and sensitivity." There was something familiar about this young actor. There was something in his pain that was reminiscent of my own son.

Heath, you had so much going for you, yet something caused you so much anxiety...so much so that you chose to overmedicate and numb your pain. You just wanted to rest.

They describe you as driven, talented, smart, lovable, sensitive, devoted... They also add in the words "anxious," "depressed," "panic disorder," and "ADD."

I pray for your life. I pray that you met Jesus and His grace. Your demons were hard to face; they kept you up all night. It's not easy on those who loved you either. God loves you, Heath. May His mercy find you and give you rest.

I wondered if characters in books and actors on television

would continue to weigh so heavily on me. I asked God if that was just my "thing" now. I knew that many realities in life would resurface the pain. It hadn't even been a year yet. Time would bring healing...or so they said.

~~~

A week or so passed and I had another intense dream. I hadn't had one since the month of Tim's passing. I guessed that I might be anxious about the one-year anniversary of Tim's death coming up. The dream came the night before Super Bowl XLII, which was another hard day to bear without Tim in our midst.

The dream started with Ted and I entering Disneyland. We were by ourselves. Our friends were waiting for us inside the park. They greeted us but were concerned that we didn't have either of our kids with us for the fun day. One of the friends lent us a child. He was a generic looking boy, around seven or eight years old. The only unique thing about him was that he held a little kitten in his arms as though it was an extension of himself. It wasn't just his pet; the kitten seemed to have the boy's same personality. It ran ahead of us as we explored Disneyland. It was very inquisitive and playful, and we kept a close eye on it. The friends we met up with did not stay with us. I remember thinking that they must really trust us to lend us this boy and his kitten for our own enjoyment. I felt grateful, happy, and blessed.

The boy and his kitten bounded ahead of us. All of a sudden, a huge, black and white cat—it was more like a monster—jumped out. It started to attack the kitten, biting its neck. We were standing in front of the castle, just before the drawbridge. The angry cat gripped the kitten and the boy as well. In desperation, I tried to fight off the monster cat, but people around me started yelling at me to stop out of fear that I would get hurt too. I didn't understand their logic and apathy. I knew I had to save the boy and his kitten; it was the responsibility I was entrusted with. I pulled the claws away. Finally, the boy and his kitten got free. I looked around and was reminded that we were at Disneyland.

I awoke from my dream and looked for my journal to write out the details. I prayed for clarity of mind to remember them.

God lent Timmy to me for a short time. He trusted me to be his mom. Together, we went down roads that led to an adventure, to a frontier to explore, to a place to believe, and to a hope for tomorrow. Yet, my son had a disease I could not fix; it attacked and continued to attack from many sides. With God's guidance, I played a part in removing Tim's pain by seeing and accepting God's will, which was to lead Tim to experience the love and grace of the Lord in heaven.

Timmy remained eternally young and playful, even as he walked across the drawbridge of life. He was in a happy place now, no longer filled with pain and anxiety. Once again, my crazy dream filled me with a sense of peace. I turned to my Bible to find more reassurance and wisdom on my journey of understanding God's perfect will.

"For He has not despised nor abhorred the affliction of the
afflicted; nor has He hidden His face from him…"
— Psalm 22:24

*"The Spirit Himself testifies with our spirit that we are
children of God, and if children, heirs also, heirs of God
and fellow heirs with Christ, if indeed we suffer with Him
so that we may also be glorified with Him."*
— *Romans 8:16-17*

*"...and they will see His face, and His name will be on
their foreheads. And there will no longer be any night; and
they will not have need of the light of a lamp nor the light
of the sun, because the Lord God will illumine them; and
they will reign forever and ever."*
— *Revelation 22:4-5*

Chapter 28

Reflections of Brotherly Love

"Do not let your heart be troubled;
believe in God, believe also in Me."
— John 14:1

February arrived. I worked on creating my third newsletter, "Heart Health." I wanted to feature a few old Valentine's Day cards from my kids, so I went looking through my treasure boxes. God, in His divine love for me, directed the arrow of grace toward a precious memento I didn't even remember saving.

I kept a large plastic box under my bed; it was one of the few things that hadn't burned up or melted in the fire—grace again. The box was filled with artwork, creative writings, and gifts made in school. They were keepsakes from my children. I sat for a long time, glancing at each piece and remembering those busy school days. Buried between construction paper and glitter, I pulled out two sheets of notebook paper that were creased together several times. I unfolded the "letter" and read the large block words written in blue, felt-tipped marker.

It was Tim's "love note" to his brother, a meticulous, thoughtful, and intentional gift that left an indelible picture of my oldest son's heart.

I sat and wept, not so much for the contents of the letter,

but because God led me to find such a precious gift. I felt His love in such a powerful way, like a big valentine from heaven. I couldn't wait to share it with Corey.

COREY,

You are fun to play with because you are my only brother.
You will always be a good brother to me
even when we fight,
like you care a lot about me,
like when you didn't want me to go in the sewers,
you were praying.
That shows that you have feelings for me.

Love your favorite (only brother), Tim

Just to clarify, my kids didn't play in the sewers. There was a wash close by to our house with a tunnel that went from one side of the street to the other; it became a frequent place for the boys in our neighborhood to play in and explore.

My boys weren't always affectionate with each other; in fact, they bickered frequently as they got older. Despite the five-year age gap that existed between them, their circle of friends molded together. Tim's closest friend, Kyle, remained one of Corey's close friends into adulthood. Corey and Kyle golfed together frequently.

"If I speak with the tongues of men and of angels,
but do not have love,
I have become a noisy gong or a clanging cymbal.
If I have the gift of prophecy,

and know all mysteries and all knowledge;
and if I have all faith,
so as to remove mountains, but do not have love,
I am nothing.
And if I give all my possession to feed the poor,
and if I surrender my body to be burned,
but do not have love, it profits me nothing.

Love is patient, love is kind and is not jealous;
love does not brag and is not arrogant,
does not act unbecomingly;
it does not seek its own, is not provoked,
does not take into account a wrong suffered,
does not rejoice in unrighteousness,
but rejoices with the truth;
bears all things, believes all things, hopes all things,
endures all things.

Love never fails…

When I was a child, I used to speak like a child,
think like a child, reason like a child;
when I became a man, I did away with childish things.
For now we see in a mirror dimly, but then face to face;
now I know in part, but then I will know fully
just as I also have been fully known.
But now faith, hope, love, abide these three;
but the greatest of these is love."

— *1 Corinthians 13:1-8, 11-13*

As I wrote in my journal about love, brothers, and First
Corinthians 13, I recalled not wanting to look too intently in

a mirror. Mornings always started out slow for me; that was one more thing I needed grace for. I didn't focus on how I did my hair or makeup. My reflection would stare back at me, the reality of loss and grief present in my appearance. I'd look for a brief moment then want to glance away, for what I felt so deeply showed upon my face. I turned to my journal.

I'm up, Lord, to face the day. The mirror is not my friend, yet it is where I attempt to put on the appearance of bright hope. The colors, the makeup, and the hairstyles won't fix my drained eyes and sagging lips. Lord, you are the only one who can and will lavish on my heart and mind. I see the true reality of physical pain. It's one more thing that has become my "new normal." Please help me today to smile and be a reflection of Your love and grace.

What was even harder was seeing that same reflection on my husband. Pain from within rose to the surface of his body.

Lord, Your will and purpose are still dim and cloudy, but I feel the warmth of the sunshine surging through. One day I will know fully. You know me fully, for I was knit together in the womb for Your purpose, and so was Timmy. You knew just how many days You numbered for him on this earth. I pray that You would allow me to understand more fully, to clear my eyes to see eternity and Your glory. Help me now, Holy Spirit, to abide in faith, in hope, and most importantly, in the sunshine of Your love.

In time, my discomfort with looking at myself in the mirror passed, as more and more of God's grace, hope, and love reflected back to me. I knew and felt the prayers of my friends that clearly mirrored God's hope.

~~~

On February 10, 2008, we received news that Ted's brother, Roy, had checked himself into the ER. He had suffered from a pancreatitis attack and was immediately admitted. After undergoing an exploratory surgery, he was diagnosed with sepsis. He was placed on a respirator in an induced coma. Yet again we were faced with hospital waiting rooms, desperate prayers, and breathing machines. In weary numbness, we hoped and prayed.

I was reminded by God's Word that love bears all things. Through many prayers and God's sovereign will, Roy improved, but it took many months for his strength to return. Our faith as an extended family grew and we rejoiced in this victory.

Love bears, love believes, love hopes, and love endures. Love also remembers.

I opened my journal in the few days approaching the one-year mark of Tim's passing. I asked God to help me see the next year through His love and perspective. I asked Him to continue to send me valentines from heaven, and to give me love and grace.

Abide in me, Lord. Your grace is love in the purest form.

~~~

The Measured

Post Hoc, Ergo Propter Hoc
(After This, Therefore Because of It)

"For You formed my inward parts;
You wove me in my mother's womb.
I will give thanks to You,
for I am fearfully and wonderfully made;
Wonderful are Your works,
and my soul knows it very well."
— Psalm 139:13-14

Given a short thread,
What with it, should I do?
Important enough to matter,
Pull together an unravel,
Tie a bead or a shoe?

For it was God who measured out
The length of this cord.
Fallen as others, twisted and knotted;
Imperfect glory.
To heaven I look toward.

What I've left, do not lay aside
For its purpose is eternal.
Add to the weave, up, over and through,
Complete a design internal;
No snag or fray in view.

See the bluer streak through the ocean,
The first fall leaf on a trail.

The spider's silvery spin,
Or the yellow and reds of a butterfly's sail.
Let this be my purpose, my cadence spirit within.

A ribbon of remembrance entwined with grace;
Let it be a pattern of peace.
Revealing glory and faith renewed
A love forever, never to cease,
Covering our hearts and souls in truth.

Chapter 29

One Year

"My soul weeps because of grief;
strengthen me according to Your Word."
— Psalm 119:28

"But You, O Lord, are a shield about me,
my glory, and the One who lifts my head."
— Psalm 3:3

A year, twelve months, an anniversary, a benchmark, *the* day… What would it mean? What would I feel? What would we do? What had God and life taught me?

God ministered to me every day, both when I cried out to Him and when I was numb to the core. He continued to bring heaven to me when my thoughts would wander to that which I missed so deeply. As I wrote in my journal, His presence and affirmation continued to minister and surround my heart with expectation and gladness of what was to come. The Holy Spirit took over my heart as I fully surrendered to Him. Despite the hard, grief-filled days, He never left me. In Second Corinthians 1, Paul spoke of being "burdened excessively, beyond our strength, so that we despaired even of life" (2 Corinthians 1:8). I was well-acquainted with that burden, but I knew God was carrying our family in His grace-giving arms.

Every character trait of God I'd been taught as a child was

now magnifying in my life as an adult. More than ever before, I knew what grace truly meant. I understood God's sovereignty, love, mercy, goodness, and most certainly, His omnipresence. I had experienced the supernatural and personal ministry from angels, songs, butterflies, and many other random things that pointed solely to God and reassured me of Tim's presence in heaven. It did not happen overnight; it was a continuing, purposeful process of seeking Him, finding the right resources, and being aware of my own spiritual and emotional states. In return, He gave me a peace that surpassed all my earthly understanding. I was brought to my knees in a powerful way of praise and thanksgiving.

I wanted to proclaim His kingdom and make His hope known. I needed to keep seeking His purposes within this framework of thinking. I didn't want to be defined as "the woman whose son died," but rather as "the woman whose God is good." I wanted to be faithful despite all I'd lost. I wanted my purpose to be solely defined by the Lord.

"Blessed be the God and Father of our Lord Jesus Christ, the Father of mercies and God of all comfort, who comforts us in all our affliction so that we will be able to comfort those who are in any affliction with the comfort which we ourselves are comforted by God."
— 2 Corinthians 1:3-4

Two types of people exist in our world. There are those who nurture hope and know the source of that hope. Then there are those who do not embrace any type of eternal hope, living only for the empty promises of the world.

I wrote down a list of juxtaposing words in my journal. I

knew which ones I wanted to pull deeper into my life—those that reflected the healing power of God.

Significant loss, *Spiritual insight...*

Anxiousness, *Peace...*

Blood, *Grace...*

Exhaustion, *Rest...*

Numb, *Sensitive...*

Absent, *Omnipresent...*

Doubt, *Confidence...*

Holding on, *Letting go...*

Mine, *His...*

Falling over, *Lifted up...*

Out of sight, *Heaven on earth...*

Empty, *Full...*

Questions, *Promises...*

Doubtful, *Purposeful...*

Needy, *Inspired...*

"For the mind set on the flesh is death, but the mind set on the Spirit is life and peace…"
— Romans 8:6

I soon realized that grief was a process of working through the bold, black letters and clinging onto and rebooting the italicized letters. The only way I would survive would be through intentional prayer, seeking God in every moment, and surrounding myself with a community that prayed for me. God's holy Word started the whole process for me. I learned that my journey closely coincided with my purpose. I relished in the fact that I was a child of God and that when He said eternity, He meant forever.

In this season of grief, I attempted to live with God's help, looking deeper and gaining insight. I looked forward to eternity with Tim and my other loved ones. Together we would praise God for His faithfulness to us and for the fulfillment of His promises. Until then, I would remain close to my family, determined to take this journey together. We needed to walk in unity, sometimes in different strides, but headed in the same direction.

The year 2008 was a leap year. February gave us one extra day. It was our choice whether we would use it to mourn or to sing His praises—grace with an extra helping of grace! On that day, I went to the garden shop and bought a bare root rose called "double delight" to symbolize the double serving of grace God had given me. I went home and spread the roots out over a mound. I watered it and tended to it. A few months later, shiny green and red leaves appeared from the dirt and buds formed. What once looked like a lifeless stick brought forth the most fragrant and beautiful blooms. God is good, indeed.

"The Lord is near to the brokenhearted
and saves those who are crushed in spirit."
— Psalm 34:18

Chapter 30

A Visit, a Voice, and a Verification

I was never close geographically or emotionally to my Aunt Margie, my mom's oldest sister. However, she began calling me regularly after Tim's death. She lived alone and had been suffering from her own chronic health issues, but she always managed to laugh and share jokes and stories with me over the phone. She possessed the wit and sarcasm that ran all throughout my mother's side of the family.

She was a gift to me in many ways. We'd get talking and I'd find myself hanging onto every word she said. It helped that the sound of her voice resembled my own mother's. Whenever I shared my grief with her, my voice would start cracking and she'd say, "You're not going to start crying now, are you?" Just the way she said it would make me pull it back together. The more we talked, the more I learned about her. She loved Kona coffee and fruitcake. She was a strong, colorful, and kind of nutty woman. She was 84 years old, but that didn't stop her from telling me all about the handsome paramedic she met after her last Life Alert call. She told me she flirted with him unrelentingly and I believed her.

She was very proud of her grandchildren and she wished she understood more about her own mother. I knew that my mother, at times, shared a similar longing. Aunt Margie talked about her bird, a cockatiel that seemed to rule the roost in her little apartment when he wasn't caged.

One evening, she called me from the hospital. The conversation quickly turned to conditions of the heart and matters of the soul. She wanted reassurance, forgiveness, and peace. We prayed together over the phone. I looked forward to driving up to see her and my cousins when summer arrived, even if it was just for a short weekend.

"I love you," I told her. I always ended the conversation that way.

"I love you too, honey. Talk to you soon."

Aunt Margie passed away on March 2, just a few days after the one-year anniversary of Tim's death.

I received the phone call from my sister while attending my small group fellowship. I grieved over the loss of yet another renewed relationship and connection with my extended family; it began and ended too soon for me. However, I rejoiced in the long, kooky, and honest conversations we had in those few months. I was thankful for her care and concern for my heart.

God is good and everything works together for His purposes.

Aunt Margie's daughter-in-law, Trudy, sent me a memento—an embroidered handkerchief and a little ceramic angel that was reaching to the sky and holding a bird. I found it most appropriate, for Aunt Margie's love in this year of mourning helped me catch my tears. It was almost like having my own mother alongside me again. Margie had reached heaven, a free bird on the wings of grace.

"Therefore encourage one another and build up one another, just as you also are doing."
— 1 Thessalonians 5:11

"Let us hold fast the confession of our hope without wavering, for He who promised is faithful; and let us consider how to stimulate one another to love and good deeds, not forsaking our own assembling together, as is the habit of some, but encouraging one another; and all the more as you see the day drawing near."
— Hebrews 10:23-25

Chapter 31

What's in a Name?

Corey thrived in school. He was consistent, diligent, and prepared, adjectives I was never able to apply to him when he was in high school. He was receiving A's in all of his classes and he even made the Dean's List a few times! I was ecstatic and beyond proud of him.

We soon approached the month of May and yet another Mother's Day—my second one without Tim. How did that many months slide by so fast with so many memories and pain? Sometimes it seemed like one never-ending day, but I knew God rose with me every morning. I hoped each day for something miraculous; many days I received just that. My eternal perspective grew wider. The hope of heaven was something I looked forward to discovering and seeing every day. I continued to write, a mandate for fleshing out my feelings.

I read through my old journals, recalling the random poetry, Bible verses, and commentary stored within. I even recorded some breaking news stories, both local and worldwide, that made me pause. I was struck by the emptiness of a world that did not acknowledge a personal and living God. In contrast, I also saw the hand of the Lord in so many things. I was brought back to the emotions, questions, wonderings, amazing grace, and insight that the Lord provided. I rejoiced in a God who knew me and provided for my every need.

The hard and lonely days found me writing, rhyming verse, and looking up lyrics to songs. Music played an important part in connecting my husband to the Lord also. It brought some peaceful noise to the hole left in our lives. God orchestrated a symphony of His comfort to fill the void of our son's absent voice.

On his off time from school and work, Corey liked getting tattoos. Tony, a close friend and tattoo artist, made that all too convenient. One day, Corey came home and proudly showed me the newest tattoo on his arm. It was in memory of his brother. I examined it closely, turning his arm and assessing every ink stain. Then, I critiqued.

The tattoo portrayed angel wings in the shape of a heart with Tim's full name written across the top. However, it was spelled "Timmothy B. VanTilburg." Yep, "Timmothy" with two M's. I cracked up as Corey's face flooded with disbelief. He was thinking the same thing I was.

How did THAT happen?

It seemed that the nickname "Timmy" got confused with my oldest son's given name, "Timothy," resulting in the misspelling. It was an honest mistake, but unfortunately it was one that could not be righted.

A few months later, I ended up writing about Corey's tattoo in a devotional format and found a place to submit it. The devotion, titled, "Spellcheck, Please," was accepted for publication in Mary Hollingsworth's, *The One Year Devotional of Joy and Laughter*.

"Can a woman forget her nursing child
and have no compassion on the son of her womb?
Even these may forget, but I will not forget you.
Behold, I have inscribed you on the palms of My hands;
your walls are continually before Me."
— *Isaiah 49:15-16*

"Be devoted to one another in brotherly love;
give preference to one another in honor…"
— *Romans 12:10*

"I, even I, am the one who wipes out your transgressions
for My own sake,
and I will not remember your sins."
— *Isaiah 43:25*

~~~

In English class at school, we read a story and I assisted my student, Michael, with his vocabulary words. The end of the week ushered in Mother's Day and my mind wandered. I felt a wave of sadness coming on, not even sure what initiated these moments. Michael was always a joy, eager to do his work. He got the dictionary and flipped to the "T" section to look up a word on our vocabulary list—*timidity.* As my finger scrolled down the page of extra-large print words, I found myself passing our vocabulary word because my eyes had focused on another…on a name. Just a few more entries down the page, the name "Timothy" was printed with the following definition, "TIMOTHY is a masculine name. It comes from the Greek name *Timotheos,* meaning 'honoring God,' 'in God's honor,' or 'honored by

God.'"

I looked up from the reference book and tears began welling up in my eyes. Yet again, God had reached down from heaven to me. He loved me and heard my quiet thoughts. He knew my aching heart deeply missed my son. This was yet another defining moment in my journey of grief, as the Lord ministered to me through Michael and a dictionary.

"The words of the Lord are pure words;
as silver tried in a furnace on the earth,
refined seven times."
— Psalm 12:6

God honored Tim by giving him amazing grace. Tim honored God by singing about that grace and knowing he received it. God honored me and confirmed again His amazing grace to me by orchestrating a school assignment, words in black and white that no one could deny. I honored God by writing and sharing the many miraculous and grace-filled moments He continued to lavish me with through my grief. I felt an overwhelming rush of peace as I recognized the work and breath of the Holy Spirit falling down on me and through me again in a classroom setting. It was truly grace upon amazing grace.

I could not define my world without the One who created me. Though the world reminded me constantly of the son I'd lost, I also felt the Lord reassuring me. I was gaining strength in the knowledge of His comfort. Inspiration on a continuum blessed me and made me keenly aware of God's presence.

In the classroom, I used tools with my students to empower them. In the same way, the Lord empowered me with His Holy Spirit, enabling me to soak in His peace. In that moment, I attempted to define my world differently, with an eternal perspective. God met me right where I was and showed me the bigger picture. Instead of mourning, I needed to celebrate becoming a mother. I needed to celebrate God's love.

"But now, thus says the Lord, your Creator, O Jacob,
and He who formed you, O Israel,
'Do not fear, for I have redeemed you;
I have called you by name; you are Mine!'"
— Isaiah 43:1

"Be exalted above the heavens, O God;
let Your glory be above all the earth."
— Psalm 57:5

Chapter 32

Donating for the Cause

The following Saturday, after Mother's Day had passed, I picked up the paper from the driveway to catch up on local news. There was one particular story of love, friendship, and compassion that caught my eye and tugged at my heart. A young woman had decided to share more than just words of love and acts of commitment; she would be donating her kidney to her friend. I continued to read about these young ladies and the kidney disease I knew so well, focal segmental glomerulosclerosis (FSGS). I felt an instant connection to them. At the bottom of the page, there was a note. It said, "For more information on Jennifer's disease, visit…" And there was a website listed beneath.

NephCure was an organization dedicated to raising awareness and support for two debilitating kidney diseases, nephrotic syndrome and FSGS. After a quick Google search, I found the contact information for Jennifer, the receiver of her friend's kidney, and sent her a message. I soon learned about a walk in Orange County that both Jennifer and her friend planned to participate in. I joined them. At the end of the fundraiser, the coordinator asked if anyone felt inspired to take up the mantle and start a walk in the Inland Empire. Without hesitation, I volunteered.

A few months passed. The regional event coordinator for NephCure planned to pick me up, take me to lunch, and help me brainstorm for the event in my area. I knew my house was hard to distinguish from the other townhouses on the street, so I waited outside, leaning against my iron gate and thinking about Timmy. I daydreamed about the walk, how many people would come, what kind of activities would take place, and what Tim would think about it all.

My angel messenger seemed in a hurry. The swallowtail rushed at me from across the street, zigzagged through the rose bushes behind me, and bounced over the fence into my garden. In that moment, I felt a sense of peace. I knew the event would go well.

The regional event coordinator and I went to lunch at Applebee's. As we walked up the sidewalk, we took note of the lilies of the Nile blooming in their lavender charm. A swallowtail followed our same path, stopping short of the entrance. We found our seats at a booth near a window where we could see the beautiful landscaping outside. Though we achieved many things in our conversation, the entertainment provided by the swallowtail outside was an added bonus.

Since that day, I've put together five walks with a small team of dedicated friends for NephCure. Our team, "Timmy's Troopers," and several others participate in our walk each year. Each walk usually takes place toward the end of October. They involve a lot of fundraising, encouraging, coordinating, volunteering, and sponsoring, but the event always blesses my heart. The people arrive, walk, and donate their money and time; they bring their children and their friends. I share with them my hope for them and their sick loved ones, as well as information on new treatments.

I didn't have those resources when Timmy was here, nor did I know the support of having families dealing with the same thing around me. I often thought about those other families. There was only one time that Timmy met someone else with his same disease.

Tim was out late that night with his friends at a local pool hall. It was well past midnight when he busted through our bedroom door, bursting with excitement about something. He couldn't wait until the morning to share his news.

"Mom, you won't believe this," he told me. "I met this guy named Jared. Guess what? He has nephrotic syndrome like me! He lives in those new houses where the strawberry field used to be. We talked all about it, the medicine he takes, his relapses…"

Tim and Jared quickly became friends. I learned that both of Jared's parents worked in the school district. In fact, I ended up working with his dad at one of my school sites.

I cannot stress enough the importance of fellowship and community to a family going through what we did with Timmy. It was something that bonded us together for a purpose and inspired both hope and empathy. It took the focus off of me and allowed me to see the bigger picture. It taught me how to use my gifts and talents; it developed my confidence and leadership.

The Bible emphasizes the importance of serving one another, as well as the need for unity within the body of Christ. It tells believers to find their gifts and learn how to use them both in the church and beyond.

"And do not neglect doing good and sharing,
for with such sacrifices God is pleased."
— Hebrews 13:16

"...and I pray that the fellowship of your faith may become
effective through the knowledge of every good thing which
is in you for Christ's sake."
— Philemon 1:6

"But as for me, I would seek God,
and I would place my cause before God;
who does great and unsearchable things,
wonders without number."
— Job 5:8-9

One year, at a NephCure walk, I met a little guy named Aidan who lived not too far from our old neighborhood. He was in the third grade, loved his pet iguana, and was a star gymnast. He had Nephrotic syndrome. He was the most precious little boy!

Sharing my experience was not (and still isn't) easy considering that Timmy is no longer here. Yet, God gave me a way to speak just what He wanted me to. He gave me the right words to bring encouragement and friendship.

This past year, Corey became more involved, adding in his own fundraising effort by sponsoring a Fish Taco Feed. Thanks to his spontaneous idea, over 100 people feasted on his catch from his fishing trips. He fried up the fish and provided a side dish of fresh, homemade ceviche. Ted and I swam with pride for Corey, his idea, and his determination to make it a reality.

Fellowship and community found its way on the seashores of Galilee, as well as along the lake of a local park. Jesus told His disciples, "Follow Me, and I will make you fishers of men" (Matthew 4:19). In that boat, along the shoreline, I found my nets filled with purpose and grace…grace upon amazing grace, that is.

P.S. After finishing up the writing and editing, and finding the perfect publisher, several years passed. I am proud to have completed ten years of volunteer work as the Inland Empire Coordinator for NephCure Kidney International. Last October, after our largest and most successful walk, I gave the reigns over to another family whose young son suffers with nephrotic syndrome. She has partnered with me in the last four years and helped to make our walks an encouraging and fun day. Timmy's Troopers will remain near and dear to my heart and I thank all of you who were ever a part of our team and came out to the walks.

Chapter 33

Illustrations of Life

The school year ended, and another summer found me with more time to write and work on projects. It was 2008, an Olympic year, and the Beijing Games were being broadcasted in our living room. The air became palpable as the familiar opening song of the summer games sounded. There was an empty space on the couch, void of a passionate spectator, opinionated commentator, and all-sports enthusiast.

Tim loved the Olympics since he first learned of their existence. When he was a toddler, we decorated his room to reflect his passion. I found posters representing different countries and Olympians. My sister, Lauren, even gifted him with a LeRoy Neiman print that we still display in our house today.

Three things happened that summer. Each one of them pointed to a particular action word—*JOLT!*

~~~

On July 22, 2008, summer school was in session. The building started shaking violently and I told my students to get under their desks. A 5.4 earthquake had struck southern California. The experts later informed the public that the epicenter was right under Chino Hills, our hometown. The last major earthquake happened 10 years prior. The 2008 earthquake left no one injured, but infrastructure damage and rattled nerves lingered in the aftershock of the morning tremor.

~~~

On July 24, 2008, a freeway car crash killed 33-year-old Christopher Laurie. He was the son of Greg Laurie, the notable pastor of Harvest Christian Fellowship in Riverside, CA and founder of the Harvest Crusades. Christopher's death stunned both his family and many who followed Greg's ministry. Christopher was a gifted photographer, graphic artist, and surfer; he was devoted to his wife and their daughter. Yet another young, active life involved in fully serving the Lord was lost.

How can we process? How can we find peace? How can tragedy strike here?

There was a popular worship song that soon became difficult for me to sing. Sometimes, I couldn't sing the words at all. It wasn't because I didn't believe them. The truth of that particular song was very real, but I was still processing and accepting it.

You give and take away
You give and take away
My heart will choose to say
Lord, blessed be Your name

I felt a sense of kinship with Cathe Laurie. I knew how to pray for her.

~~~

On the last day of July 2008, well after midnight, I was awakened by my groaning husband.

"I'm not feeling so good," he informed me. He had cold sweats and said his chest was hurting.

"Do you think it's because you missed your blood pressure medicine today?" I asked.

"No. This feels a little strange. My arm hurts too."

"Do you want to go to the ER?" I questioned.

"I don't know. Let's wait..." A minute went by. "Yeah, I think we should go," he said.

After 24 hours and a transfer to a bigger hospital, the diagnosis revealed that Ted had suffered from a mild heart attack.

What is "mild" about a heart attack?

The doctor performed a coronary angiogram to get a better look at where the blockage was. He needed to determine if Ted needed any other procedures, such as an angioplasty. My new friend, Deanne, a woman I'd just met in the weeks following my return to school, accompanied me in the waiting room.

Ted's results came back, revealing that he had two blockages. As a result, the blood flow went around and through another artery, called a "collateral," causing the body to have to compensate. He did not need surgery.

Thank you, Lord.

A "collateral" is defined as an alternate route, a way around something, a change of direction, a side road, a road less traveled.

Training and finish lines, routines and struggles, life and death, pain and suffering, shifts and realignments, heartaches and heart issues... All of these things continued to rumble in our lives—in everyone's lives, actually. We were presented with two choices. We could either live defeated, grumble, hide under our desks and in our work, hesitate to take a detour of healing, and stay stifled. Or, we could depend on God to lead us in a miraculous way around the damage.

We would never forget the pain and grief, but we knew we could take all of our experience with us to those we meet along the journey. The pressures of life always even out in the security of sufficient grace.

"Therefore, having been justified by faith, we have peace
with God through our Lord Jesus Christ, through whom
also we have obtained our introduction by faith into this
grace in which we stand; and we exult in hope of the glory
of God."
— Romans 5:1-2

During the summer of 2008, Beijing beguiled, Chino churned, the Laurie family felt loved, and hearts continued to heal. I wrote a story called, *The Adventures of Fuller and*

216

Lester: A Story of Love and Encouragement, which took first place in its category on FaithWriters. Then, I began to put the words of the story into pictures. I purchased high-quality colored pencils and set out to work. On each page, God gave me a clear picture of how the characters would look and interact. I used my own garden for reference. The story began to take on new life as each page filled up with color and personality.

Sketching out my pain, I presented the rough drafts to the Lord. In each page of time and memory, I began to see the hope coming to the forefront from the background of grief.

Slowly, but with a sense of perseverance, in a studio displaying my portfolio of hopes and dreams, my own color began to appear. At one time, things seemed so gray. I was used to seeing the shadows more than the light. However, God brought out the watercolors, providing brushstrokes of hope for me to mix and apply to my heart and prayers. Every piece of paper I wrote on or illustrated I chose to give back to Him. Sometimes I offered Him sheets that I'd already wadded up and tossed into the trash. That happened when I forgot for a moment who promises healing and hope. I realized that when I tried to do things myself, without a model, the scribbles and drippy messes did not show a clear picture of grace at work. Nevertheless, God always sees something, a potential masterpiece, through His comforting and merciful eyes.

I will continue to give God my broken crayons and my dull pencils. I will continue to ask for His inspiration, to show me what He has for me. He is my light, a contrast to the darkness of grief.

"For God, who said, 'Light shall shine out of darkness,' is the One who has shone in our hearts to give the Light of the knowledge of the glory of God in the face of Christ."
— 2 Corinthians 4:6

Chapter 34

A Purposeful Job, Then Retirement

As my story and illustrations began to take on life, something else formulated in the mind of an acquaintance— a woman I'd recently met while attending my small group. Linda, through her own road of suffering and searching for purpose, attended a seminar that inspired her to want to step out and be active in serving. She was aware of my desire to write and my need for support. She was also a former editor and lover of stories. She proposed that, together, we start a writer's group as a form of another small group at church.

"Sounds interesting and fun," I said.

Who's going to attend and what are we going to do? Read our personal stuff? Learn grammar?

I was totally clueless as to what this new gathering would entail, but I found Linda so interesting and trustworthy.

We put together a format for the class. Following church protocol, we set up a sign-up table in late August. To our amazement, several writers signed up. We met in the church library at first, but we eventually moved to a bigger classroom as the group expanded. We called our unique group the Aspiring Writers' Forum.

In our group, each member learned about and developed their skills in the processes of writing, editing, rewriting, and submitting. In our second year, we self-published a Christmas advent booklet; all the proceeds went straight to youth camp scholarships. It was an absolute joy to collaborate with other writers and make a camp experience possible for those who needed it. It was a great honor seeing our words illustrate the miracle of the coming Savior.

Every Wednesday night, our group meets for an hour and a half class. We journal on questions pulled from the previous Sunday's sermon and share our reflections in complete authenticity. In our group, we experience true worship, fellowship, tears, and laughter. Sometimes we pull together nerdy grammar stuff, but we always find a way to laugh and learn new things. Toward the end of the evening, it is our custom to listen to several submissions by group members. There are in-progress fiction novels, anecdotal stories of life experiences, and even some epic poetry. Critiquing, which is always done in a positive way, leaves us looking forward to the next chapter, encouraging the growth and strength in the confidence of the writer.

A continuation of grace upon amazing grace, the gifts of God added a layer of comfort and purpose which encouraged me to stay diligent in my emotional health and spiritual wellbeing. He pulled me gently from spilling my words onto pages for only His heart to sharing my heart with others. Today, I continue in leading others to do the same. Within that whole process, grace swirls full circle in a prose of purpose. As I recall some of my favorite verses, I know these truths affirm God's personal touch in my healing and hope.

*"Now faith is the assurance of things hoped for,
the conviction of things not seen."*
— Hebrews 11:1

*"Every good thing given and every perfect gift is from
above, coming down from the Father of lights, with whom
there is no variation or shifting shadow."*
— James 1:17

~~~

A large official looking envelope came in the mail one day in late September; it was addressed to Tim. Since it had been a year and a half since my son's passing, my curiosity found me opening it up. The title of the letter, underlined and in bold letters, read, "The 15-Minute Retirement Plan: How to Avoid Running Out of Money When You Need It Most." I read through a few of the bullet points, feeling a wave of melancholy coming on as I thought about Tim working a job longer than a year.

The letter continued to explore the idea of what they considered every person deserved to have—a carefree, active, and rich life. I paused, knowing that we don't really deserve anything. The word "grace" lined itself up with my thoughts again. Tim was no longer tired, having retired into the arms of his heavenly Father. I was confident that he was now living a carefree and active life. He wasn't rich according to the world's standards, but he was rich in the rewards of heaven, having received an unending account of abundance.

The letter gave an incentive for sending back a response

and requesting more information—Titleist Pro V1 golf balls. The text continued to appeal to the idea that golfing was probably "Tim's idea of heaven!" (Yes, it really said that!) My guess was that he received this because he put himself on a mailing list at a pro shop somewhere. According to Tim's earthly life, they most assuredly got that one right. But according to heaven's new resident, Tim might just tell you how to spend that 15 minutes preparing your heart for something that lasts past retirement—eternity.

"For the Scripture says, 'Whoever believes in Him will not be disappointed.'"
— Romans 10:11

~~~

I found another treasure in my keepsake box beneath my bed. At just nine years old, Tim knew too much already about the broken world we lived in. For a school assignment, he wrote five changes he wanted to see in the world (no drugs, no gangs, no plane crashes, more in my allowance, and to be better). He wrote not just for his own little world to change, but he saw beyond himself in the first three points. He switched his thoughts to himself in the last two, attributing to himself more responsibility and more hope.

You've got all five points now, Tim. You're in God's gang now, flying on wings like eagles and rich beyond measure. God's allowance called "grace" bought you and redeemed you from this broken world. You're so much better off now, for you reside with God.

God clearly states in His Word that He is always with us,

in every time and every season of our life. How thankful I am for His promises!

> *"Listen to Me, O house of Jacob,*
> *and all the remnant of the house of Israel,*
> *you who have been borne by Me from birth*
> *and have been carried from the womb;*
> *even to your old age I will be the same,*
> *and even to your graying years I will bear you!*
> *I have done it, and I will carry you;*
> *and I will bear you and I will deliver you."*
> *— Isaiah 46:3-4*

Chapter 35

Blogs and Clogs

"For You have delivered my soul from death,
indeed my feet from stumbling,
so that I may walk before God
in the light of the living."
— Psalm 56:13

The weeks began to fly by, but the grief never dissipated. It became a part of who I was now, a different way of seeing the goodness of God. People say things become easier over time. For me, the grief I was experiencing and the phrase "easier over time" seemed like polar opposites. All the dimensions that make up the human core remained a challenge every single day. Some days, I was stronger in a certain thought, task, or emotion than others. God allowed me to understand a bit of His plan and a certain peace naturally followed from His Spirit ministering to me. Like a door slightly ajar, I began to see a glimpse of eternity I never sought before. Many think I over-spiritualize things because of my pain, but I think that's exactly what God *wants* us to do. He wants us to see Him through our tears. I remained emotionally and mentally aware of His presence, and hope continued to surge within.

I prayed a lot, asking God to pull it all together. I felt His strength and His inspiration in everything around me. Things did not become easier for me; I simply became more determined and inspired to not just live with my incredible loss, but to travel outside of it and explore the options of it as much as I could. I breathed, moved, and found worship in every moment, actively living in the presence of God. In doing just that, I felt closer to Tim, nearer to heaven. I desired a holier intimacy with the Lord.

I continued to journal every day, co-lead my writing group, and started to write more devotional type messages. As I pressed further into God, I started to share a bit more about my experiences and emotions.

Eventually, my cousin-in-law, April, sent me a text message, asking, "Have you considered starting a blog?"

Considerable Thoughts found a space on the internet soon thereafter, yet another dimension of expression for my love of storytelling. My first post was made on July 4, granting me a new kind of independence. I had to brave the idea that once I hit the "post" button, my thoughts and words became global.

My first post was a poem about the passing of Michael Jackson. April congratulated me by writing my first ever comment. I found blogging challenging, yet incredibly fun. Sort of like fireworks, they are posted and then preparation for the next one begins.

~~~

I often found myself thinking in rhyme, wanting to tell a story in that genre. In February 2009, the second anniversary of Tim's death approached. I walked numerous times past the clogs in the corner of the stair landing. Grandma and

Grandpa VanTilburg gifted Timmy with the wooden shoes when he was three years old.

"...and having shod your feet with the preparation of the gospel of peace..."
— Ephesians 6:15

I sat down and wrote this poem to capture the shoes, my son, and his legacy. God granted me peace and I sought to walk in it each day.

~~~

Little Wooden Shoes

Little wooden shoes, what story do you tell?
Of a blond boy who wore you with pride.
Such tiny feet fit, the soles nestled deep
Did tread with unseen Sandals at your side.

Now sitting on the third stair landing,
Shouting loud with colors bold and bright.
The protection of something so tender,
Ten toes and a heritage by sight.

A gift to a grandson so special,
From the Netherlands, your father's birth home.
The land where gardens ever splendor;
For wading and walking on the loam.

Little wooden shoes for a party,
For dress up, a costume fair?
A perfect match with suspenders and knickers.

Red and green socks to add to the flair.

A pose, a picture well taken,
Of times spent in the earth clogs.
Little boy, firstborn wearing
Little wooden shoes carved from poplar logs.

Scuffed and scarred like the soul of the wearer;
Outgrown, but longing for time.
A purpose of protection from stepping
On invisible things in mud and slime.

Little wooden shoes, no stretching mandated,
So they stayed on a shelf for the while.
The Sandaled footsteps followed,
In time fit him with grace and style.

But, little wooden shoes, your purpose still lingers
Adorned in bright yellow and red fray.
To serve as a reminder of pleasure;
Of youth, a carefree, bright day.

Young Dutch boy who wore you proudly,
For family and homeland ne'er forgot.
Now serve us in silence; we will fill you
With hope and the small feet in our thoughts.

Chapter 36

Turning to Face the Light

"…and His face shone like the sun…"
— *Matthew 17:2*

The summers found me drawing, writing, listening to a lot of music, growing closer to special friends, and loving the feel of dirt in my hands. I no longer saw my counselor.

I was healing by God's grace, by my intentional seeking of Him in the tragedy, and by the knowledge of what I knew of His character. He is good. His love is perfect and eternal.

The yard in our new place lacked "curb appeal." Since I loved to garden, I worked on bettering the soil, planting roses, and carving out sections in the backyard for veggies and flowers. I also found the perfect place to bury some sunflower seeds—right outside my kitchen window. With just a little attention, they sprouted and grew quickly. Their whimsical nature and bright color lit up the backyard. I loved to linger for a few moments here and there in the kitchen, watching them, caught up in their amazing stature and strength. Most mornings, my devotion and prayer time took place where I could enjoy coffee, the view of the sunflowers, and the promise of a good day.

~~~

Sunflower Song

Out my kitchen window, I planted to see,
Giant sunflowers, swaying so softly.
Dug around the marigold plot,
Up they arose along the fence, a great spot.

Harvesting seeds from last year's crop,
The dried, crusty bloom saved from rot.
A few to the birds, gathering all the rest,
To plant this year; sort of a test.

Emerging, up and up with speed.
Staked, planted firm against their own weight and need.
The bees gather 'round more than before,
I spotted a mantis, praying for more.

In my observation, today God speaks,
As I stood by the window thinking on summer weeks.
The first and largest now hangs its head in grace,
For it has served its purpose, leaving seeds in place.

The others stand 'round with multi-blooms on stock
At watch over the yard, no hesitant balk.
Knowing they serve with whimsy and purpose,
But their days are numbered, preparing to leave us.

I think of my son, and his own shining short season,
So like the sunflower, deliberate with reason.
Planted and nurtured to leave memory seeds,
Continuing to plant for all the heart's needs.

My hope, that one will grow in your yard,

A bright yellow flower to always stand guard.
A reminder of seasons, some short, some long,
But a memory of grace told in a sunflower song.

~~~

Sunflowers… They stand tall, their giant heads turned to face the sun, revolving with it as it moves across the sky. I, too, took my giant, broken heart and faced the Light. He blazed with love and purpose into my life, providing new seeds to nurture. I found His hope in creation, delighting in it. I drew pictures for my stories and started taking my camera out into the garden.

In my new, grieving heart, I pursued moments, looking deeper and with more intent at everything around me. I thought I might hear God more, feel Tim closer, or recall a memory. While all of those things happened, the best result was that I recognized God's relentless pursuit of me. In my heart and in my mind, I felt His deep love for me as I surrendered my sadness to Him every day.

The miracle of grace began in my heart long ago. Like a seed needing further nurturing, and with a pinpoint of faith at the center of my soul, God expanded upon the first recognition of my need for Him.

Jesus said in the Sermon on the Mount, "Blessed are the poor in Spirit, for theirs is the kingdom of heaven" (Matthew 5:3). His heart is for those who come to the dirt plot wanting and needing to see beauty. He sifts, removes the hard dirt, and buries seeds of grace deep in the soft, rich soil of our hearts. He plans out a beautiful sequence, a template for His children's lives that reflects His glory. In His Word, we are told to ask, seek, and knock (Matthew 7:7-8). He wants us to participate in His garden.

In nature, we can see a replication and beautiful pattern in many things. It's called the Fibonacci design and the evidence of it is seen in shells, pinecones, butterfly wings, succulents, the insides of fruit, and sunflowers. This pattern of grace has captivated me over and over again, in my life, in circumstances, in random things, in nature, and in His Word, swirling around in perfection. Hope has captured me at the broken center of my soul. God's thumbprint is stamped upon every precise detail, giving me an identity, not as a mother who lost a son, but as a mother who knows that following the difficult path God has laid before her will result in grace upon amazing grace.

On that path, peace becomes infinite and I am able to see eternally. I breathe out grief and take in a perspective filled with a soul-directing promise. It is a promise that shows me how sunflowers turn and face the light, and how a caterpillar transforms into a magnificent butterfly. When I look toward heaven, I am reminded of that place where all of God's children live with Him in perfect glory, forever and ever. Time and time again, God's Word affirms my heart.

"Behold, I will do something new,
now it will spring forth; will you not be aware of it?
I will even make a roadway in the wilderness,
rivers in the desert."
— Isaiah 43:19

PLAYLIST XIV

Son-shine

1. "Things Left Unsaid (Acoustic)" — Disciple
2. "Say" — John Mayer
3. "Let It Die" — Foo Fighters
4. "What I've Done" — Linkin Park
5. "Love Remains the Same" — Gavin Rossdale
6. "Leave Out All the Rest" — Linkin Park
7. "The Heart of Life" — John Mayer
8. "Take My Life" — Jeremy Camp
9. "Lost at Sea" — Jimmy Needham
10. "Clarity" — John Mayer
11. "The Shadow Proves the Sunshine" — Switchfoot
12. "Pocketful of Sunshine" — Natasha Bedingfield
13. "Believe" — Mainstay
14. "From Sunrise to Sunset" — Paul Wright
15. "Voice of Truth" — Casting Crowns
16. "Smiling Down" — Pillar

Chapter 37

Stages of Life and a Road Trip Rhapsody

"Nothing can seem extraordinary until you have discovered what is ordinary. Belief in miracles, far from depending on an ignorance of the laws of nature, is only possible in so far as those laws are known."
— *C.S. Lewis, Miracles*

I knew I could not look away or dismiss the Divine. I didn't want to take for granted the amazing things in this world. Butterflies continued to greet me in opportune times, when I was thinking, praying about something, and especially when I was in need of encouragement. If it wasn't a butterfly, God gave me a Bible verse or a song. I knew God was listening to me. He provided comfort and I continued to feel His presence all around me. I felt like I was a completely different person after experiencing true intimacy with God every single day. I wanted more of Him. The Apostle Paul's letter to the Roman church highlighted that very thing—a promise for those who desire intimacy with God.

"...and hope does not disappoint, because the love of God has been poured out within our hearts through the Holy Spirit who was given to us."
— *Romans 5:5*

In the fall of 2009, I started working at a new high school.

The four fantastic years I spent with my student, Michael, opened my eyes and heart to special needs students. God affirmed me in this job. I looked forward to work each day, going to a new school and meeting a new student. I knew God's plan would continue wherever He led me.

Often, Michael blessed me with a few words about Timmy being in heaven, watching down on us. In his innocent, big heart he believed that though life was a little challenging, everything was good. He'd often remind me, "God is so big!" Then he'd chuckle and return to whatever I had him working on.

My own dad rarely talked about God. However, I had a strong memory of him singing the song, "He's Got the Whole World in His Hands." I definitely knew that God's goodness guided my every step and that I wasn't alone in my walk; I had the Lord and the people He placed in my life. My life became a dichotomy of pain and hope, yet God remained omnipresent and omniscient in His grace upon amazing grace healing moments.

"Great is our Lord and abundant in strength;
His understanding is infinite."
— Psalm 147:5

Corey finished up his two-year program at ITT Tech in December of 2009; the celebration of his accomplishments highlighted the end of our year. Family and friends joined us as he walked across the stage and received his diploma. He raised a hand and nodded toward heaven, knowing that Tim was smiling down at him with pride.

~~~

The summer of 2010 arrived and my sister, Lauren, decided that the two of us needed to go on a road trip. She loved adventure, always the family historian and genealogy investigator. We headed out to northern Arizona, where she planned for us to step into the Old West. My grandfather's and other family members' tombstones were hidden on a bluff overlooking the desert floor. Afterward, we headed to St. Johns for a second overnighter.

We gathered for a continental breakfast in the dining area of our motel. One seemingly regular customer—a truck driver, I assumed him to be—sat at a table talking to an older African American woman who appeared to work for the motel. They talked about local business for a minute and then she went about her work, cleaning tables and straightening up the dining area. While she worked, she sang.

I can only imagine what it will be like
When I walk, by Your side
I can only imagine what my eyes will see
When Your face is before me
I can only imagine

My sister was the first to say something. "Oh, we love that song. It has a special meaning for us."

She came to our table radiating a sweet love for her Lord and Savior, smiling as if she knew exactly what we meant. She looked right at me, and without me having to say a word, she started to sing another praise hymn, one that might be sung in an old country church. Her voice gave me goosebumps.

We finished our meal and she went about her business, but I couldn't get her soft, southern voice out of my head. She communicated hope while worshiping the Lord as she worked. Yet again, I felt His presence as we prepared ourselves to head out into a forgotten land of cowboys and sheepherders, rusted farm equipment and horizons that seemed to stretch on forever. In the distance, the White Mountains loomed, gray storm clouds gathering at the top.

After our visit to St. Johns, we headed across the Painted Desert toward Flagstaff. We arrived in the early afternoon, which deemed enough time for us to enjoy our dinner and a stroll through town before sunset. The quaint town of Flagstaff was set in a beautiful valley surrounded by forests. It was a college town, boasting of Northern Arizona University, as well as a historical railroad that ran right through the main hub of the town where many shops, eateries, bookstores, and coffeehouses were situated. The town offered a comfortable ambiance, serving as a great place to meet up and hang out after studying. Balmy weather with soft breezes wafted through the ponderosa pines as we strolled through the town, walking off our dinner. The sidewalks were busy with college students, shoppers, and more than a few out-of-towners like Lauren and me.

We came to an intersection. Lauren, a little ahead of me, pressed the button to cross the street. I heard the music. I stopped and turned to look at the group of young people sitting along the sidewalk in front of the corner building. They strummed their guitars and tapped on their percussion instruments; a single guitar case sat open for donations. One red-bearded musician met my glance.

"What's your favorite song?" He asked me with a smile.

I didn't even have a chance to answer him.

At the light, Lauren turned and watched our interaction. The musicians prepared to play a new song—my silent request.

He started to sing.

> *Amazing grace, how sweet the sound*
> *That saved a wretch like me*
> *I once was lost, but now I'm found*
> *Was blind, but now I see*

I stood paralyzed with awestruck wonder. I took in every word of his melodious voice. The light began to change, slowly becoming darker outside.

"Come on, let's go," Lauren said to me.

I wasn't going anywhere. The man started to sing the next verse.

> *'Twas grace that taught my heart to fear*
> *And grace my fears relieved*
> *How precious did that grace appear*
> *The hour I first believed*

Continuing on, he sang the familiar, extra verses provided

by Chris Tomlin, a contemporary, Christian singer-songwriter and worship leader.

My chains are gone, I've been set free
My God, my Savior has ransomed me
And like a flood His mercy rains
Unending love, amazing grace

I began to speak to him about the song. I told him that those exact lyrics were the last words my son said—the ones he sang to me before he passed away.

The man only smiled and said, "Yes, I know that."

I don't know what my sister was thinking, but I could tell she was anxious to leave. However, I knew I just had some kind of supernatural encounter. I wanted to take a picture to remember the moment, but my cell phone was dead from taking a lot of pictures and my camera was in the car. Lauren and I started walking again. Once we got about a block away, I stopped and turned around. I just had to get back to the corner again. I needed my sister to take a picture.

Ten minutes later, we returned to the street corner and the band—all five of them—were gone. The spot that was just inhabited sat empty. I looked across the street and down the block, but they were nowhere to be found. Yet, somehow, they remained everywhere.

Just like grace itself, the song was amazing and unending. It was a promise that unlocked the chains of pain and drew me into God's hope. I was completely set free to live in His grace. Timmy knew what this felt like. He, by God's grace, got it. Grief might've been a locket I wore around my neck, but I could no longer let it be a chain around my feet. Because of the promise of the Holy Spirit who dwelled inside of me, I had received freedom into hope.

"Now the Lord is the Spirit, and where the Spirit of the Lord is, there is liberty."
— 2 Corinthians 3:17

"So if the Son makes you free, you will be free indeed."
— John 8:36

Reminding me of God's promise, a new song played continually on road trips and in backyards, in a full house of church worshipers and in the classroom with my students. He never ceased reminding me that He was near, whether through the wings of butterflies or bearded, singing angels. Grace upon grace directed me to stop when the world said go and told me to go when the world said it was impossible.

"Do not neglect to show hospitality to strangers, for by this some have entertained angels without knowing it."
— Hebrews 13:2

"Sing to the Lord a new song; sing to the Lord, all the earth. Sing to the Lord, bless His name…"
— Psalm 96:1-2

Chapter 38

Trusting
(Along God's Continuum)

"He is your praise and He is your God, who has done these great and awesome things for you which your eyes have seen."
— *Deuteronomy 10:21*

The months, seasons, and "Timmy weekends" continued to move me further into God's grace, granting me inspired moments of peace. I had a greater understanding of God's purpose for me; it kept steadily building and revealing itself in and through what I was writing, seeing, feeling, and believing. "God is good" became the mantra of my days.

The writing group met faithfully every Wednesday throughout the regular season— September through May. Meanwhile, another ministry started up at the church. Coffee Break was a women's group that met once a month, coming together for coffee, dessert, and an encouraging story from a member of our own congregation. I learned the importance of sharing a testimony of faith through the hard and unexplained seasons of life. Through the broken and lost, the heartbreak and the diagnosis, transparency and growth revealed themselves again and again. Every woman that came left encouraged, knowing that God was infinitely good. I joined the prayer team for the ministry. I knew one day my own story would be told, as the pieces of the journey became clearer.

In October 2011, I launched my second blog, *Friday Footnotes*. I purposefully named it after a day of the week to hold myself accountable to posting every Friday. Each blog post included a scriptural heading and anecdotal musings, ending with a prayer of thanksgiving. With this blog, I had a very specific goal—to strengthen my writing while sharing the hope of the Lord. This blog was different from my first in that it continued to keep my mind and eyes focused on the Word of God. It was applicable to everyday life and world events, because I knew that God was relatable and loving. He was continuing to reveal His love and purpose for me in my writing, allowing me to relate Him to others.

Facebook helped me do this more spontaneously. I enjoyed posting encouraging things, sharing pictures from my garden and of my family, and connecting with friends from the past and present. It was a great tool for communication. My hope was to use the platform as yet another way to share good, encouraging things.

Once I finished the illustration of my children's story, *The Adventures of Fuller and Lester: A Story of Love and Encouragement*, I began dreaming about getting the story and its artwork published. It was a dream I held so close to my heart, but I still had so much to learn about writing and publishing.

~~~

It was a Sunday night… I remember the way God nudged me, encouraging me to reach for courage. During this season, Ted and Corey both worked out of town, seven hours away from home. They'd both left a few hours before, leaving me alone to fend for myself for the rest of the week. My cell phone rang, presenting me with a challenge.

"Are you emotionally ready and able to tell your story at Coffee Break for the month of April?" Linda asked me. That was just a few weeks away.

I knew this day had been marked at some point on God's timeline, but God's timing and my timing didn't seem to be on the same page. However, I knew His was perfect—mine, not so much.

I had shared my story before with a few trusted friends, but only in bits and pieces. Now, I was being asked to present it in front of a crowd of over 150 women, most of whom I didn't know. To speak about my son, from his birth to his passing, and then the aftermath...

What about all the questions they might ask me? Am I ready for this, Lord?

I wrote a cryptic poem in my blog that week after the Lord gave me a verse—one that I still hold very close to my heart. On February 27, 2012—the five-year anniversary of Tim's passing—I sat outside and sipped my coffee. A drizzle greeted me on that cool, winter morning. I heard a few doves cooing on a nearby roof. I opened my Bible and turned to Psalm 27. It was there that I found the strength to speak.

"I would have despaired unless I had believed that
I would see the goodness of the Lord

in the land of the living.
Wait for the Lord;
be strong and let your heart take courage;
yes, wait for the Lord."
— Psalm 27:13-14

~~~

The Day of the Living

Dark of day-night
Weary warriors leave the bunker
To gather and hunt.

Alone, with dreams blanketing,
Tucked into trust,
Sun surges up
Grabbing day-promise
As the last one thousand eight hundred and twenty-six
days…
Horizon.

Expectation rouses the slumber,
Its loud voice proclaiming a chorus.
Listen carefully, "Do you hear it?"
"This is the day…!"

Rejoice.
Remember.
Reconsider.
Resurrect.
Rekindle a blaze.
Never relinquished to ash.

Grace pours out hot-warm,
Sweetened in love…
And Grace-words,
They flash across the touchscreen of my heart.

"We never knew him but…"
"We miss him too."
"Your God—He is good!"

(Can my God be so good?)

Same God.
Same Love.

The sky-fountain showers thirsty earth.
Fellowship gathers 'round,
Shelter through the storms.

God-tilled, mother-teared soil yields harvest.
Prepared bounty.
Hope messages:
"Set aside seeds for spring planting."

"Today is the day you ask of me, Lord?"

"This day?"

(Spirit on Pilgrim's pathway swoops down.)

"It is time to walk among the living,"
He coos in the Psalm page of the day.

Choose Life.
Choose to Trust.
Choose to Live.

One thousand eight hundred and twenty-seven days.
My grateful heart ticks toward Eternity's reunion.
"Walk in the Land of the Living...
And be glad in it."

~~~

The date, April 2, came quickly. I'd spent the previous two months preparing my testimony for Coffee Break. My time had come to be obedient to share my story of heartbreak, disappointment, healing, comfort, and hope that I'd experienced over the last five years.

Speaking in front of people had never been easy for me, even with my experiences in sales, retail, and teaching. My nerves were ramped up due to both my emotions and the large audience that awaited me. I worked with Linda to get my testimony on paper and I practiced the presentation. I bought myself a new outfit and invited my sister and many of my friends who didn't go to church.

On the drive to church, a song came on the radio—"Song of Hope (Heaven Come Down)" by the Robbie Seay Band. I had heard the song before, but this time the lyrics were speaking to me differently, directly. I felt the Holy Spirit's presence giving me extraordinary courage and hope. Once again, I knew God orchestrated this song and these lyrics; I felt Him stirring in my heart.

All things bright and beautiful You are
All things wise and wonderful You are
In my darkest night
You brightened up the skies
A song will rise, I will

Sing a song of hope, sing along
God of Heaven come down, Heaven come down
Just to know that You are near is enough
God of Heaven come down, Heaven come down, yeah

All things new, I can start again
Creator God, calling me Your friend
Sing praise my soul, to the maker of the skies
A song will rise, I will

Sing a song of hope, sing along
God of Heaven come down, Heaven come down
Just to know that You are near is enough
God of Heaven come down, Heaven come down

Oh, sing a song of hope, sing along
God of Heaven come down, Heaven come down
Just to know You and be loved is enough
God of Heaven come down, Heaven come down

Hallelujah, sing
Hallelujah, sing
sing, oh Hallelujah, sing

We gathered, ate, fellowshipped, worshiped, and then I told my God-story, my faith and grace story, my son's story, my family's story. It was a story that continued on, a never-ending story of hope all the way into eternity. God reminded me every day in miraculous ways of that hope. He used the sunrise, ocean tides, rainbows, and butterflies. I eagerly pursued Him. I looked intently on His face, fixing my eyes in expectation. The reminders of His promises always appeared suddenly, sometimes in the quiet and other times in the chaos and confusion. His love for my family proved steadfast time and time again. I was completely confident in who His Word said He was—the absolute truth and the hope in the turmoil of my life.

Five years ago, Ted and I sat in the waiting room of the ICU, flu-ravaged and twisted up with emotion, surrounded by family and true friends. The vigil began. Minutes passed into hours. The sun rose and set several times. We waited. We visited. We prayed.

We watched Tim's breath rise, our anticipation following suit, only to dwindle with despair. Grace's song opened the heavens.

A surgeon came along and accepted the challenge when no one else dared. Grace hummed the second chorus of its song. Ted—my soulmate in this journey—walked down the long hallway toward me. He was wretched with pain as he looked into the eyes of my breaking heart. I could sense his effort to try to grab back the words he wished he never had to say. Grace sang another chorus.

The world turned dark and the earth slid out from under my feet. My heart and brain crashed together in a head-on collision—fatal, but not final. Amazing grace swept up the debris and set my world on an axis, spinning toward heaven.

In those five years, amazing grace surrounded me. Amazing grace comforted me with understanding, fellowship, renewed hope, and purpose. God held my thoughts and emotions in His gentle, merciful hands. I felt His love for me. I knew Tim had found rest and peace in eternity. One day, I would see my son again. It was a promise that had been affirmed to me over and over. It motivated me to give Him praise and pay attention to His words more than ever before. He allowed me to see the miraculous and supernatural every single day, underlining His grace to me, deleting my despair, editing out the emptiness, and writing eternity across my heart. As God continued to heal me, I continued to want to seek more of Him and serve Him with a renewed joy.

His Word encouraged me to stay focused and reminded me of His promises of eternity. Yes, I missed my son every day, even as I read the delicate pages of my Bible, but I knew I needed to continue on in God's plan.

"I will bless the Lord at all times;
His praise shall continually be in my mouth."
— Psalm 34:1

"Through Him then, let us continually offer up a sacrifice
of praise to God, that is, the fruit of lips that give thanks to
His name."
— Hebrews 13:15

"Rejoice always; pray without ceasing; in everything give
thanks; for this is God's will for you in Christ Jesus."
— 1 Thessalonians 5:16-18

PLAYLIST XV

Timmy's Five-Year Memorial Mix

1. "Vice Verses" — Switchfoot
2. "Lovesong" — Adele
3. "Souvenirs" — Switchfoot
4. "Restless" — Switchfoot
5. "Never Be the Same" — Red
6. "Where I Belong" — Switchfoot
7. "The Healing Has Begun" — Matthew West
8. "Us Against the World" — Coldplay
9. "Every Teardrop Is a Waterfall" — Coldplay
10. "If We've Ever Needed You" — Casting Crowns
11. "I Run to You" — Lady A
12. "Running to You" — Newsboys
13. "Born Again" — Newsboys
14. "Always Enough" — Casting Crowns
15. "As Long as I'm Here" — Brandon Heath
16. "How He Loves" — David Crowder Band

Chapter 39

Brighter Days

"If nothing ever changed, there would be no butterflies."
— *Wendy Mass*

Summer break arrived and with it, warmer weather. I was given the gift of intentional gardening in this season; it was therapeutic and rewarding. On June 17, 2014, I began a new journal to help the process of writing this memoir.

I returned home from a morning workout with my close friend, Christina. I entered through the side yard, taking in the morning view of my new landscape. Earlier that spring, I'd planted a butterfly garden. Now, the wildflowers stretched toward heaven, their bright, yellow faces singing their own song to the busy, outdoor sky.

When I walked inside, I saw my laptop open on the dining room table. It was surrounded by a few journals, notes, newsletters, and my Bible. It was that very spot where I'd recollect and sort through memories and feelings of grief. It was there where grace served itself up as the main dish, where I broke bread with the Divine, where the sweet nectar of salvation communed with the promise of eternity and the heavenly dessert of hope.

I'd completed the preface and first chapter the day before. That morning, I would begin the second chapter. In hindsight, that was the hardest one to write. I stopped short of finishing to watch the butterflies in my garden.

Never, not in any of my days, had I seen a butterfly like the one I saw that day. It was still, seemingly not in a hurry. Its wings were spread out like a stealth B-2 Spirit, refueling on a bright, yellow and orange flower. I had my phone handy, so I took several pictures of it. Because it was a type of butterfly I'd never seen before, I was curious of its name. I felt the presence of the Holy Spirit confirming that the words I wanted to write in my manuscript were for His glory. I just needed to be still and feed continually on His goodness through this process.

Lord, allow my words to color the darkness, draw in hope, and give flight to Your purpose...all for Your glory.

I went inside and Googled the size, shape, and color into the search bar. The search took me a while because I wanted to be exact. Finally, two options popped up—the mournful duskywing or the funereal duskywing. They were very similar, but after reading the descriptions of each in more detail, I concluded that the butterfly in my garden was a funereal duskywing.

How fitting, God, to give me a butterfly to match up with the next chapters of my memoir. Your hope has flown into my life—undercover, yet dutiful to obey.

When I went back to writing, music and God's Word played an important part in motivating me. The Holy Spirit led me to a specific verse.

"After you have suffered for a little while, the God of all

grace, who called you to His eternal glory in Christ, will Himself perfect, confirm, strengthen and establish you."
— 1 Peter 5:10

I read it several times, then I listened to the song playing in the background; the lyrics, just like the butterfly, were preparing me to move and to write and to share His healing.

I'm not about to give up
Because I heard You say
There's gonna be brighter days
There's gonna be brighter days
I won't stop, I'll keep my head up
No, I'm not here to stay
There's gonna be brighter days
There's gonna be brighter days

I just might bend but I won't break
As long as I can see Your face

When life won't play along and right keeps going wrong
And I can't seem to find my way
I know where I am found, so I won't let it drag me down, oh
I'll keep dancing anyway

I'm gonna move, move
I'm gonna move, move
I'm gonna move
I'm gonna move

— MercyMe, "Move"

Several other experiences during the writing process only

served to strengthen me and pull me closer to the God who I knew redeemed all things.

> *" '...but let him who boasts boast of this, that he understands and knows Me, that I am the Lord who exercises lovingkindness, justice and righteousness on earth; for I delight in these things,' declares the Lord."*
> *— Jeremiah 9:24*

Nature and the Holy Spirit became one in my life, and I delighted in the perfect way God brought it to me when I was willing to seek Him. God was all about making His presence known in my life.

Chapter 40

"Doing a Good Thing, Doing Well..." Or So I Hear

I received another speaking opportunity at a women's fellowship at a small church who was pastored by some family friends. Cathy, the pastor's wife, wanted me to share with her ladies about journaling and how it helped me grow closer to the Lord and find peace. I invited two of my closest friends, Melody and Marcia, to come along for support.

As Marcia and I were preparing to leave the house and pick up Melody, a swallowtail butterfly flew into my view. It was as though the Lord was giving me a hug and saying, "You're doing a good thing. Take courage, for I am pleased."

After a successful day of pampering and inspiration, the women's ministry blessed everyone with fellowship and encouragement. Once I got home, I felt exhausted. I went to lay down for a nap. God continued to minster to my thoughts in another special dream.

I slept quite soundly for three hours, but I awoke to someone shaking my ankle.

"Wake up, wake up," she said. "I am proud, so proud of you. You are doing so well."

The touch on my ankle felt so real; I could still feel the warmth of her hand. I sat up immediately, realizing it must have been a dream. Yet, I was so sure that I'd heard her voice and felt her hand on my skin. I could never forget my mother's touch...

God, You knew I needed that reassurance. Thank You.

"For thus the Lord God, the Holy One of Israel, has said,
'In repentance and rest you will be saved,
in quietness and trust is your strength.'"
— Isaiah 30:15

~~~

To this day, my garden has continued to be an ever-changing, fun hobby that I thoroughly enjoy. God is omnipresent, but He seemed to faithfully shine His glory and speak to me in my garden. There was something about the garden that caused me to think about what heaven would be like.

"The flowers have already appeared in the land;
the time has arrived for pruning the vines,
and the voice of the turtledove has been heard in our land."
— Song of Solomon 2:12

Chapter 41

Aftercare Atmosphere

Just turn around and I'll be there
I'm moving into your atmosphere
— TobyMac, "Atmosphere"

The school and church season of 2013-2014 began, and my writing group started back up. New faces and seasoned veterans gathered around to write and share. That year, I began to share the chapters I'd written for this memoir with the group, submitting my soul for critiquing in a safe and trusting place.

By November, the first four chapters had been read by the group. The fifth chapter was next on the agenda for submission. If you don't recall, that chapter had several paragraphs that mentioned Timmy's ICU nurse, D'Anna. She truly went above and beyond her role as a nurse to bring comfort and care to my son and our family. It was through her love and compassion that I knew God orchestrated His servants in supernatural ways for the benefit of His children.

The next evening, I felt the need to share with her that I'd written about her and was planning on showing the chapter to my writing group. I sent her a Facebook message...

Hello. I feel I should tell you something.
This summer, I started to put together my
memoir and write a book about Tim, his

*passing, my journey through grief, and
God's healing process.*

*I've written 22 chapters and I am sharing a
little at a time with my writing group only.
Last night I read Chapter 5. It's about the
few hours we had with Tim after his passing
and your caring for him while he was with us
and after he passed. I've only used your first
name. I hope when I share this with you,
you will feel my love and appreciation for
all you meant to us and all your kindness
during that time.*

She replied instantly…

*That's amazing. I was just talking
about you and Timmy yesterday, as a
matter of fact. I was asked in a job
interview what was the most profound
moment in my career, and I spoke
of you and Timmy.*

I messaged her back…

Really?!

*Oh, wow… I am overwhelmed.
Let me know when you want to read
the first five chapters. I will send them to you.*

Her response came quickly…

Thank you. It was truly a blessing
for me to be a part of your lives.
I would LOVE to read it.
I couldn't imagine your grief.
You are an example of strength.

To close our conversation, I told her...

God is my strength, thank you.

I couldn't believe it! On the same day I had decided to read the fifth chapter to my writing group, she had used Tim and me as an example of a "profound moment" in a job interview!

Our hearts crossed paths once in an ICU, and now they intersected again in the aftercare of memories that are for our good and wellbeing.

"Do not fear, for I am with you;
do not anxiously look about you, for I am your God.
I will strengthen you, surely I will help you,
surely I will uphold you with My righteous right hand."
— Isaiah 41:10

~~~

A few weeks passed and I shared again. Chapter six was about the planning and presentation of Timmy's memorial service, and Jason Andrews, the pastor who officiated the service. As I mentioned before, he had been Tim's youth pastor.

Our writing group met in a different building at the church than all of the youth activities and men's studies, meaning I never saw Pastor Jason on Wednesday nights. As I prepared to leave our weekly meeting, he walked in the door as Linda and I started to exit.

"Hi, Jason," Linda greeted him. "Coleene shared tonight in her memoir about you and your role in Tim's memorial."

I never see Jason on Wednesdays. I just talked about him… I just shared Tim's memorial service chapter… Lord, this is You…

I finally managed to say something. "I am still so grateful how that service came together and how much this church means to me," I told him, holding back my emotion.

"I've done a lot of memorials, but to this day, that was the greatest selection of music for any service I've done. I still listen to that CD," Jason said, affirming me and filling me with memories of songs, sadness, and the supernatural.

Once again, I was confirmed by the Holy Spirit that my unfolding story contained more chapters to come. I continued to experience more grace upon amazing grace.

God spoke His love loudly to me. His gracious comfort continued to fill me, and I was very aware of it. I took note of it in the aftercare of loss, grief, wounds, wonder, healing, and thanksgiving. His promises in Scripture spoke to this very thing.

God spoke His love loudly to me. His gracious comfort

continued to fill me, and I was very aware of it. I took note of it in the aftercare of loss, grief, wounds, wonder, healing, and thanksgiving. His promises in Scripture spoke to this very thing. Can you fathom that God's Word is a love letter written to the world, but also to your personal heartaches, wonders, and desires?

"You will make known to me the path of life;
in Your presence is fullness of joy;
in Your right hand there are pleasures forever."
— Psalm 16:11

Chapter 42

"Let There Be Light"

In my life, butterflies became the symbol of transformation of something into beauty and hope. They appeared all over my story of healing; with them in mind, I put pen to paper and began writing the next chapter. On that particular afternoon, the warm summer sun was still ablaze in the sky. I sat in my writing space with music on and notes ready. The ambiance was perfect for writing.

Ted would be home a little later than normal because he was working down near San Diego. I liked writing in a quiet house.

Eventually, the setting sun seemed to tell me, "Goodbye. Here is the twilight to keep you company."

My words were flowing as I told the story of "Sunrise Swallowtails." Later, Ted walked in the door, worn from a long day and his commute. He glanced at his awaited section of the couch where he liked to relax. He adjusted the blinds to block out the sun, as our house faced west, then he went upstairs to take a shower.

I sat at the dining room table and finished up the chapter. If I looked to the right, I could see into the living room where Ted would soon retreat. The sun made its way through, but the adjustment of the blinds contained the light to a single beam, blazing at an angle across the room.

I stood and stretched, feeling an overwhelming peace. God had filled me with the words to write and I understood the beauty that came from living for Him and His hope. I turned and walked into the living room, following the beam of light with my eyes. My heart was open wide.

The room, almost dark, except for the one beam of light, seemed void of almost everything else. Where the molecules of illumination hit the opposite wall, I saw it radiating.

"The people who were sitting in darkness saw a great light, and those who were sitting in the land and shadow of death, upon them a light dawned."
— Matthew 4:16

The wall, spotlighted now, held something else of significance. Right above where the light hit, there was a shelf that held the ashes of our son, Tim. Suddenly, the holy beams seemed to morph into very identifiable icons of hope.

I called to Ted upstairs to quickly come down and see before it changed in movements of time and space.

When Ted came down, he turned his head sideways as I outlined the shape for him. The dust particles, visible and swirling around in the brilliant beam, were forming wings that belonged to either a butterfly or an angel. For a moment, the lines became less dramatic, softened as the shape began to split a bit. Then they grew brighter as a new form came back together—a heart with three circles coming from one side as if they were dancing upwards. I grabbed my cell phone and took pictures at each interval.

Ted thought it was cool, but he wasn't as enraptured with it as I was; he went about his business of making dinner and relaxing. It wasn't until I pulled up the pictures that I took on my computer that he really understood the power of the moment. He needed a fresh perspective—an eternal perspective.

"I pray that the eyes of your heart may be enlightened, so that you will know what is the hope of His calling, what are the riches of the glory of His inheritance in the saints..."
— Ephesians 1:18

The light continued to move past the wall and shine into the dining room. I watched it hit the very chair that I sat in just a moment ago writing the pivotal chapter that marked the beginning of my healing process. As if wanting to be touched by Him, I moved my body to sit again in the chair and absorb the warm beams of light that were directed by a loving and powerful God to shine into the darkest of places of my life.

"God saw that the light was good;
and God separated the light from the darkness."
— Genesis 1:4

"Then Jesus again spoke to them, saying, 'I am the Light of the world; he who follows Me will not walk in the darkness, but will have the Light of life.'"
— John 8:12

Chapter 43

My Favorite Part of Heaven

"For the gate is small and the way is narrow that leads to life, and there are few who find it."
— *Matthew 7:14*

"In My Father's house are many dwelling places; if it were not so, I would have told you; for I go to prepare a place for you. If I go and prepare a place for you, I will come again and receive you to Myself, that where I am, there you may be also."
— *John 14:2-3*

My parents both played golf. When she was in her fifties, my mom, who was always up for a challenge, donned a pair of snow skis for the first time. I knew that sports kept people active and enthused, whether they were a participant or a spectator.

With his kidney disease causing frequent absences and relapses, school sports were not an option for Tim. However, you could always count on him being in the stands, rooting for his high school team, and making friends with the parents of the players.

Once he graduated from high school, Tim's true passion was found in the game of golf. In younger days, sports filled our calendar for both boys. Tim started out team sports in baseball, playing until he reached the "Majors" level in Little

League. Corey played baseball for a little bit, but soccer soon dominated the schedule for all three of the boys in my life. Ted volunteered as a coach for many years, refereed, and then served on the league board.

I will never forget the day that Timmy picked up a check from working a job of hanging drywall for a short time. He had no idea that the job offered "prevailing wage." His check for just a few days of work was over $800! He went straight to the sports apparel shop in our neighborhood and purchased his own set of clubs and a golf bag. He was now a legit golfer!

Memories of his golfing days lined up in my mind. He worked at El Prado Golf Course in Chino, one of his favorite places in town. His schedule needed him to be there very early in the morning. I'd drive him down through the dairies on Euclid Avenue in the morning fog. We'd sing to the radio together to wake up. Tim would spend the day returning carts and cleaning up after golfers and tournaments, most likely talking to as many people as he could about their game and experiences. That job was heaven to him—the rolling greens, the water hazards, the sand traps, the doglegs, the locals, and the pro shop.

In my grief of missing him, I tried to imagine that he was playing golf in heaven. I tried to imagine what he'd be wearing and the smile on his face. One day, I found myself writing a story about it. It was a comforting dialogue about a heavenly game on the greens of paradise. It was reminiscent of the movie, *The Legend of Bagger Vance*, which starred Will Smith and Matt Damon. A scene from the movie replayed in my head.

"What I'm talkin' about is a game. A game that can't be won, only played," Will Smith's character, Bagger Vance, said.

"You don't understand," replied Rannulph Junuh, played by Matt Damon.

"I don't need to understand," Bagger challenged. "Ain't a soul on this entire earth ain't got a burden to carry he don't understand, you ain't alone in that. But you been carryin' this one long enough. Time to go on, lay it down."

~~~

I wasn't quite sure if I was in a dream or not. Rhythmic tones of bagpipes faded in and out in the background... Or was it a machine breathing? I intentionally listened, trying to feel everything. My senses cooperated as if they had been opened up to a new level, fine-tuned to full capacity. I smelled the color green—fresh and earthy, but somehow more intense than I could imagine. I couldn't get enough of the scent. I felt so at peace, but there was also an excitement building up inside of me. It felt as though I was about to experience something wonderful, something I'd always been hoping of, something vaguely familiar.

My eyes searched my surroundings. I knew where I was...or so I thought.

Hallowed ground...

The hills, slightly undulating, were all shades of green;

there were colors I'd never seen before. Behind me, I saw the iconic stone footbridge over the Swilcan Burn. Further in the distance, I made out the silhouette of the clubhouse. I could hear the telling whispers of the greatest legends of golf swirling around me like a heavenly gallery. St. Andrews… It had to be. I bent down to touch the grass, which was glistening like emeralds.

Is this a dream come true? Did someone grant me my last request? It certainly would be just that…to play a round at St. Andrews Links in Scotland.

I was in the country of highlands, whiskey, and tartan kilts. It was the land that my mother's ancestors farmed and pillaged. Most importantly, this land birthed a passion. There was a story I'd heard that went as far back as the 12th century. According to legend, Scottish fishermen found relaxation and a bit of competitive fun by playing a game with a pebble and a piece of driftwood. The player that hit the stone the furthest claimed victory.

Did they mark the pebble somehow to identify it?

For centuries, golf had been a national pastime in Scotland. In the 1500s, golf became the game of kings, played in courtyards and higher learning cultural centers. Now, I was at St. Andrews, the oldest, most historic course there was.

The crowd parted and I saw someone. A golfer approached me, his caddy at his side. I was suddenly aware of my own physical body. I wondered why I felt so alive amidst this surreal experience. I wanted to absorb it all. I recognized the golfer immediately, garbed in his colorful, stylized outfit.

"Hello, young man, I'm glad to be partnering with you today. Have you had a chance to practice a little and get warmed up? Don't let this flat-looking course fool you. We will encounter many surprises along the way."

"Excuse me," I said, shaking his hand. "Are you real or is this heaven?"

I looked at his caddy and recognized the love that had surrounded me for as long as I could remember. He was my caddy as well—in my good games and my not-so-good games. He was the carrier of all my burdens and the keeper of my official scorecard. I knew Him. He smiled.

"Well, son," Payne Stewart said, "whenever someone arrives here, they have to place their ball down on the first tee shot of this everlasting course. I would say this section, called St. Andrews, is a perfect representation of the many courses available around here. Do you feel good today?"

"Um, yes, sir. I feel better than I have ever felt…in my whole life, actually."

"Breathe deep, son. Let the breeze fill your lungs. It's the answer to all your prayers. And remember, we've got that 17th hole called the Road Hole. You might just figure out what the plans are for you here once we get there. You already won; you're with us. Your crown and trophies are waiting for you, so let's play!"

The caddy drew near and handed me a driver. I noticed that His palm was scarred. I touched Him and I suddenly knew everything. Reaching inside my shirt, I felt for my own scar, the one that went from my collarbone down to my stomach. It was gone, vanished, mended.

I was Home.

Since then, I've played every day all across heaven. Sometimes bagpipes accompany me in a chorus of angelic praise, but all the hallelujahs and applause are not for me. St. Andrews has remained my favorite part of heaven... Payne and I partner up a lot.

My approach shots took a lot of practice on earthly golf courses, but now I had the greatest instructor in the game of eternity—the greatest caddy there ever was. The first time I made it on the green, it truly felt like amazing grace. It was as though I was given a mulligan, a chance to make everything right again. That was the purpose of the caddy; He made everything right for everyone, for all of humankind, on an old, rugged cross set up on an undulating hill called Calvary.

I believed and I listened to my caddy, Jesus Christ, for His instruction. He knows the Game of Life as the Creator. When it's your time, you can be confident that your swing will be a hole in one.

> *"As you walk down the fairway of life*
> *you must smell the roses,*
> *for you only get to play one round."*
> *— Ben Hogan*

Chapter 44

An EXecutive Letter

Dear Friends,

It's me, Tim. I'm here to eXplain heaven. Well, not really eXplain, but rather eXtrapolate more since I got here before you and am waiting for you. Let me eXpress in words and convey a true eXpression.

Because of eXtenuating circumstances and problems that were becoming eXponentially greater on earth, God in His sovereignty did what was best for me. You know I hate waiting. God eXpedited everything, giving me a whole new, perfect body! Not only can I inhale deeply, but I can eXhale too. Heaven's oXygen is so sweet, like chocolate-covered strawberries. My pain is totally eXtinguished; my anXiety is gone forever!

I hang out now in an eXtravagant mansion that eXceeds the limits of all earthly architects. On top of that, I'm right neXt to Gramma Joyce. Mom, remember when I eXtemporaneously sang "Amazing Grace" to you? Yeah, I knew you needed that for the days to follow. I love how God did that; it was a gift for both of us! eXtremely cool!

He loves you all so much! God's love eXtends more than you could ever imagine. I get to watch how He works through other messed up people like me, eXterminating darkness from their hearts in ways only He can. He gets the glory.

In heaven, I'm in the company of eXtroverts. God has special plans for us gregarious, unreserved eXperts. I spent twenty-siX years eXpounding on what I thought was important, but now I have the grace of heaven and nothing matters eXcept humility and forgiveness. I let Him eXterminate the ugly and now I am an eXample of Him to the world. It's an eXplosion of peace; that's an oXymoron I know, but it's true.

To all of you on the eXterior of His eXcellence, ask Him to fill you with His eXtraordinary love. You'll know why I am so eXuberant once you do. No one can really eXperience heaven until you arrive, but at the eXact moment the Holy Spirit comes to live in your heart, you can get a taste of it.

Don't put God in a boX! Heaven is only the destination; it is not the reward! I am full of eXultation, singing, praising, eXuberant in eXpressive joy. Being with God is eXhilarating!

Be still… That's what they used to tell me, but really…be still! Feel those eXtra-sensory whispers from the Creator. Capture those X's and O's eXclusively for yourself. Heaven is eXceptional because no one comes to the Father eXcept through His Son, Jesus. God made us eXactly in His image. We messed it up, but God made an eXemplary plan. On earth, many of us get eXhausted trying to be perfect. Some don't feel as though they have the eXtended time. I didn't.

Use your time wisely, prepare your heart, and ask God to lead you to the correct eXit when your time comes. While on earth, live with eXpectation of all He does in and through you. Believe in the eXtension of His grace upon amazing grace.

Thank you for letting me eXtol my Savior. Thank you, God, that You loved me so much that You eXpended Your own time in heaven to come to earth and live a perfect life, only to be brutally eXecuted for us. You are God, You eXtinguished death, and You rose on the third day. I know I only had a mustard seed of faith, yet You gave me an eXemption through Your grace. Life can be full of disappointment, hardship, and unmet eXpectations, but God never fails. In all things, be thankful and know that He is good, eXcellent, and eternal.

Sincerely,

Timothy, eXpatriate of earth and citizen of heaven

"For it was fitting for Him, for whom are all things, and through whom are all things, in bringing many sons to glory, to perfect the author of their salvation through sufferings."
— Hebrews 2:10

Chapter 45

Reflections

"What we have once enjoyed we can never lose.
All that we love deeply becomes a part of us."
— *Helen Keller*

As I reflected back on my process of healing, I knew that it was a journey that was nothing short of miraculous. I had so much to be grateful for. From the moment I became "conscious" again, grief and loss were a part of me. It wasn't something I could just get over or move on from. However, I knew my hope and wellness remained, and my faith and trust in the Lord endured.

With eyes opened to all He prepared to give me in His comfort, I took those steps forward. Nine years later, as I remember our son and the months after his passing, I never could have imagined all the supernatural glimpses of heaven and powerful rushes of spiritual insight I've continued to receive. The only response I could fathom is to marvel at His love and the likeminded friends He has brought me.

I am so grateful for His Word; it has given me so much hope and peace every single day. I am also thankful for the opportunities of ministry and growth I have received in the fellowship of the church. I now live in hope and victory because of the promises and love of my Savior who gives me strength for all my days. He has given me an abundant serving of grace upon amazing grace.

*"But we do not want you to be uninformed, brethren, about
those who are asleep, so that you will not grieve as do the
rest who have no hope."*
— *1 Thessalonians 4:13*

*"'For I know the plans that I have for you,' declares the
Lord, 'plans for welfare and not for calamity
to give you a future and a hope.
Then you will call upon Me and come and pray to Me,
and I will listen to you.
You will seek Me and find Me
when you search for Me with all your heart.'"*
— *Jeremiah 29:11-13*

As I shared my experiences throughout the process, both orally and through social media, I would occasionally hear back from those who knew Timmy and were coming to terms with his passing. There were three specific stories I knew the Lord wanted me to share—to provide a glimpse of Tim from other perspectives. The first, Debbie Osterman, a dear friend of mine, is a mother herself. The other two, Stephanie Flanagan and Tiana Colgate, were some of Tim's closest friends.

~~~

Because he was an active high school student in the same circle of friends as my own daughters, we saw Timmy frequently at our home on Sunday nights for additional fellowship. When my husband, Mike, and I got to know Ted and Coleene, we realized we had a lot in common and bonded with them quickly. Even after my family moved to a different church for a while, our connection never faded. After several years, we returned to our original church home and instantly found camaraderie with our old friends. Seeing Ted next to Coleene's side, worshiping together, filled Mike and I with joy.

One day, as I drove through town to pick up my grandkids, Chris Tomlin's song "I Will Rise" played on the radio. I sang along, praising Jesus in my car.

I will rise on eagles' wings
Before my God fall on my knees
And rise, I will rise

I turned the corner and that's when I saw Timmy. He was leaning against the signal post, one leg up, smiling. I *knew* it was him. I started shaking. I pulled into a parking lot to calm down. I wanted to call Coleene, but I didn't have her number, so I called the church office instead in hopes that they'd give it to me. I had to share with her that Timmy appeared to me while I was singing "I Will Rise."

I called but got her voicemail, so I left a message explaining what happened. There was one feeling I felt so vividly—peace. It was overflowing, flooding, never-ending, promise-filled peace. The knowledge of it literally took over my body and brought me such joy. I knew, without a doubt, that Tim lived eternally in heaven with Jesus. I knew that God had blessed that hyperactive kid that never stopped talking with His amazing grace. Although I was sad for my dear friend's loss and pain, I felt true joy from the Lord. I knew that if I trusted in Him for the impossible, He could make all things possible.

When I finally got the chance to talk to Coleene at church, she informed me that the day I saw Timmy was his birthday. She and her family were out of town, celebrating with a "Timmy Day."

In sharing this story with her, she also informed me that the front cover of Tim's memorial program contained the verse that Chris Tomlin received inspiration for "I Will Rise" from...

"Yet those who wait for the Lord will gain new strength;
they will mount up with wings like eagles,
they will run and not get tired,
they will walk and not become weary."
— Isaiah 40:31

Timmy, I know you are walking, running, and soaring in heaven. Thank You, Lord, that Your grace reaches out from heaven and fills us with the promise and hope that You are our cornerstone and crosswalk. You are our green light to a heavenly home. Thank You, Jesus, for allowing me this precious moment with Timmy on his birthday. Thank You for the opportunity to soar through trials with peace and understanding.

Never put God in a box. He is able to do above and beyond what we could imagine, according to His goodness and will.

Align with Him, friends, and know this same peace.

— Debbie Osterman

~~~

I was on my way to high school and I saw this kid, obviously much younger than me, walking with a backpack that had the name "Timmy" written across it in Sharpie.

How cute! I thought.

It turned out that my mom and his mom knew each other. Later on in life, they became very close friends. Naturally, I became friends with Tim, who was only two years younger than me. After high school, we saw one another at a local hangout called Kelly's. We spent a lot of time there shooting pool and singing karaoke.

Tim liked to talk, but I did manage to get a few words in; we had a lot of great conversations. He was funny, smart, and also serious at times. He concerned himself with many things in life. I always tried to boost his confidence and help him see the positive side of things when he was discouraged. I knew he had health issues, but I didn't know the extent. In my mind, we were just enjoying life in the here and now.

When I got married, we held the wedding and reception in a friend's backyard. Tim and Coleene were our "wedding coordinators." They made sure everything went well that day, which was a lot of work. I will never forget the time that he took to do that for my husband, Chris, and me.

Tim worked for my mom for a while, soliciting photographs for her booth at the Ontario Mills shopping mall. One day, he was "missing in action." My mom eventually learned that a live TV show was interviewing random people to get funny responses. Well…you guessed it. Tim managed to get himself on camera; Bob Eubanks got a taste of Timmy's charm and precociousness. He certainly didn't need any coaching.

Tim, I can picture you now, a cute, little blond boy with "Timmy" written across your golden robes. I can picture you bouncing off the clouds in heaven, wanting that one-on-one time with God. I miss you, Tim, but I'm so glad that God coordinated all He did to bring you to Him.

Peace out, Timmy…

— *Stephanie Flanagan*

~~~

Timmy,

Usually, by the time you're in high school, this name is shortened to "Tim," but somehow, the name "Timmy" just fit him. He was smaller in stature and possessed a rambunctious personality. We had been friends since early elementary school, and we lived in the same neighborhood growing up.

Tim was feisty and sometimes not so nice to other girls…you know how boys can be. But Tim and I, we had an understanding. He knew I wouldn't put up with his…*stuff*. He let his guard down around me and knew he didn't need to impress. I got to know the real Tim. Our relationship remained like that throughout the many years we were friends.

From a young age, I understood that Timmy felt the need to be "bigger" in all the ways he could. It was like a protection mechanism, to be funny, assertive, and noticed. He always made me laugh; he was definitely the class clown, but not always the teacher's joy. We had a special bond I knew would last a lifetime.

He may have been small for his age, but he always protected me. One night, when we were out, some guys were trying to hit on me, annoying me, and making me feel uncomfortable. Tim stepped in and rescued me, then got me home safely.

On another occasion, we ran into each other at Kelly's. A group of us left together to do something else, not wanting the night to end. We thought we might drive up to the mountains. At one point, "Tiny Dancer" by Elton John came on the radio. Not too many seconds passed, and we were all singing the song. It was just like a scene in the movie, *Almost Famous*.

That was the last time I saw Tim.

Sometimes, when I am in a situation and I need a friend to talk to, I pray and think about my grandma and Timmy in heaven. I know they're both watching over me. Many might not believe this, but one night, I asked for a sign that they were both still with me...and all of my electronic things lit up!

Tim was a great friend to me. We had a lot of love,

understanding, and respect for one another from the day we met. He liked to play hard and have fun. Maybe that wasn't so good for him, but he couldn't help himself.

Tim, you probably know everything now because you're in heaven. Sometimes life gets really hard for me, and people on earth aren't so understanding. I could always talk to you about the good things and the bad. I still do. Please ask God to keep guiding me because I know He is good and knows what's best. It is a comfort for me to know that you are waiting there, that I will see you again. Whenever I hear "Tiny Dancer," I still think of you.

In *Almost Famous*, the hero, William, is given an opportunity to hang out with a band called Stillwater for several days. William is a young writer and rock 'n roll enthusiast who wants to get a story on Stillwater for a magazine article. After a while of living with the crazy musicians, he knows that he should probably get back home. Finally, the band loads back into their tour bus and hits the road for the last time; they are quiet and reflective. The song "Tiny Dancer" begins to play on the radio. One by one, each character jumps into the song, singing the lyrics and feeling the redemption the song is bringing to their group.

William turns to Penny Lane and says, "I have to go home."

Penny, smiling at William, says, "You *are* home."

Tim, I know that rock stars didn't kidnap you, but I do know that you needed to get home, to the place where redemption waited for you. Now, your mom writes the story and we live in the memory of the music you left in our souls.

Sing to your heart's content, Tim. You've certainly had a lot of practice at Kelly's on karaoke nights. Now, I know you're totally in tune.

Hold us closer, Tiny Dancer...forever.

— Tiana Colgate

~~~

To those I asked to share your own grief-grace story with me, thank you.

Blake, our best friend; God sent you a shooting star at the moment you prayed and hoped that your mom, coming from an Eastern religion, accepted Jesus as her Savior after reading the Bible in Japanese, her native language. God's promise and grace spread across the heavenly realm.

Joyce, your mother's uniquely spelled name was painted brightly on the side of a building as you left her memorial service and headed for the reception. You asked her to give you a sign that she was with God and in seeing those large letters, God bestowed grace for your eyes and peace in your heart.

Jeff, your mother suddenly succumbed to a brain aneurism, but on that very day God gave you an opportunity to thank her from the bottom of your heart with words you never spoke out loud to her. It took time to heal, but God's grace gave you peace to continue honoring both your mother's memory and the God who granted you gifts in music to give Him praise.

Debi Lynn, God graces you with feathers to remember your mother and guide your path in wisdom.

Dawn, a song loved by you and your husband, plays at opportune times to remember the love you had together.

Randi, God sent you a beautiful double rainbow when your heart ached after learning of the death of your closest childhood friend from cancer.

Don and Margaret, a king's crown graces soul and skin as you remember your sweet son, Ryan, taken tragically from you in a motorcycle accident. The theme of a cancelled baby shower, "I Can't Wait to be King," took on a whole new meaning. That baby was born, named for your son, and in that there is always hope.

My dear friend, Eileen, your memory tree, planted in your son Christian's honor and his favorite verse, John 3:16, continues to give you hope that one day you will be reunited because you believe and God is good.

"For God so loved the world, that He gave His only begotten Son, that whoever believes in Him shall not perish, but have eternal life."
— John 3:16

Epilogue

As I reflect on the three summers I spent writing this book, I know I must start at the very beginning, in the Word of God.

"For of His fullness we have all received,
and grace upon grace."
— John 1:16

Fullness... It's the feeling you get after you've eaten way too much and the buttons on your jeans are strained. It what happens when you top off your gasoline and it runs down the side of your car. It's when you pack everything you think you'll need for a weekend trip in a small suitcase...and then some. It's when you're nine months pregnant and can't see your feet anymore.

Things stop when they are full...or, in the case of a pregnancy, they release. I am releasing this story to you so that you can fill your own hearts. My desire is that these words flow into your own grief and fuel your desire to be filled with the Holy Spirit, the Word of God, and amazing grace.

We have all received... Christ came in the form of a human baby. Mary released Him to God from the moment she was told that she would conceive the promised Savior of the world through the Holy Spirit. Jesus was never hers; He belonged to God. He *is* God.

He is omniscient. He is willing to forgive, to grant us pardon, and to fill us with His love, hope, and the promise of eternal life. We belong to Him, yet He gives us the freedom to choose His love.

I think often of the last words my son spoke to me.

Amazing grace, how sweet the sound...

Grace upon grace... We must pray in gratitude for every special gift we encounter, those that open our souls to receive and believe that God's plan is good. We must change the way we think, the way we seek, and the way we listen for His voice. It is a posture of surrendering which makes room for God to continue filling. His grace saves us from ourselves.

Every day I pray in thanksgiving for the things I discovered yesterday, the grace I was given for today, and the hope I have for tomorrow. My desire for those reading this is that they be continuously filled up with the "upon grace" part. It is His sustaining, watching, waiting, redeeming grace that gathers us in His arms and moves us forward. It is a grace that overflows the cup. It is a grace that is not meant to be kept, hoarded, or stored away. When we receive this grace, we should share it with others. It is a blessing to watch grace flow into someone else's space, filling up and spilling out again.

God's transforming grace carries us through seasons of suffering. With just a mustard seed of faith, a willingness to be still and know His peace grows within. He is faithful to grant grace that sheds the skin of self-doubt, unworthiness, and mediocrity; it is a grace that produces new skin.

We wait and pray, weep and mourn, seek and ask, absorb His wisdom and recognize His voice. We trust His process and continue believing.

Eventually, God will tell us, "It is time, My beloved child. I've got you. I always have."

We will emerge, shaking off the old self. We will hear, see, and feel encouragement. We will spread our new wings and fly, dipping and gliding, soaring high on the very breath of God.

~~~

Whoever is reading this, you are beautiful, worthy, and a part of His plan. Everything that happens to you is for His good; you can trust that because *He* is good. One day, He will give you wings like eagles. You will not grow weary. You will rejoice forever in the presence of the almighty God. Everything is for His glory.

"These things I have spoken to you, so that in Me you may have peace. In the world you have tribulation, but take courage; I have overcome the world."
— John 16:33

PLAYLIST XVI

Timmy Mix 21: Soul Thoughts

1. "Good to Be Alive (Hallelujah)" — Andy Grammer
2. "The Time of My Life" — David Cook
3. "Believer" — Imagine Dragons
4. "Savior's Shadow" — Blake Shelton
5. "Hills and Valleys (The Valleys Version)" — Tauren Wells
6. "You Never Let Go" — Matt Redman
7. "Wonder" — Hillsong UNITED
8. "I'm Not Who I Was" — Brandon Heath
9. "Higher" — Unspoken
10. "Oh My Soul" — Casting Crowns
11. "Call It Grace" — Unspoken
12. "Different (Acoustic)" — Micah Tyler
13. "Control (Somehow You Want Me)" — Tenth Avenue North
14. "Heaven's Here" — MercyMe
15. "Remind You" — Andy Grammer
16. "Grace Will Lead Me Home" — David Dunn

Who doesn't love to view visuals for just a bit more understanding? I've made that available on my blog! You can find pictures that accompany some chapters at coleenevantilburg.blogspot.com.

Acknowledgments

To my husband, Ted, and my son, Corey, I thank you with all my heart for your support, love, and belief.

Linda Boutin, thank you for being my writing partner and co-leader. Thank you for your unrelenting encouragement that God's plan can grow from two unlikely characters into something neither of us could imagine. Thank you for inspiring me every day with your strength.

To all the members of the Aspiring Writers' Forum. Thank you for listening to me, reading my chapters, helping me with editing grammar, believing in me with this project, and keeping tissues close by.

Thank you, special friends…those who are likeminded and faith-driven, those who God brought graciously beside my family and me. From waiting rooms, living rooms, classrooms, dining rooms, and coffeehouses. From journals to manuscripts, from simple prayers to war room cries, from the chrysalis of grief to His magnificent wings of hope; thank you for your encouragement and love which have guided me and moved me forward to believe in God's plan for all things. You have suffered with me and celebrated with me. We have cried, remembered, laughed, and prayed together. The Lord knows and hears our weaknesses. He sees where we are broken. He is stronger than anything that wants to steal our joy. I look forward to the many days we will spend together rejoicing in His victory.

Lord, thank You for teaching me and showing me how to focus with a new perspective. I am now able to see Your gifts of grace everywhere. It is a perspective that points me toward heaven and all of eternity.

Just call it what it is… Call it *grace*.

Without the body of Christ, in particular, my church, Chino Valley Community Church, this healing process and the discoveries I made about grace and my own purpose could not have been as clear or as certain.

To Pastor Jason Andrews and his wife, Tiffany, you two loved on me when I faced difficult parenting issues with Tim in his high school days and I know you prayed for him. He loved you. Enjoying a game of golf with you, Jason, might have been a natural pastime in these current days of busy schedules. Thank you for coming alongside us in the many hospital stays and your steadfast dedication at camp and youth group, for guiding Tim to have a relationship with the Lord. I especially thank you for helping us plan his Celebration of Life. I know you remember Tim with the song choices I made for his service; you seemed to really understand where I was coming from. Thank you for remembering and commenting on the many funny times, and the laughter. You saw us both at our worst and now God sees, one on the sanctifying road and one home, the Glory Road.

I chose some very special friends to pre-read my manuscript. I'd like to acknowledge and thank them for their wisdom and input, each one a bit different.

To Blair Aldworth, educator and co-worker, and one who can empathize having lost her stepson, your positive encouragement and generosity inspire me.

To Steve Atkinson, my friend and my grief counselor, you always ask the right questions. Your care and your grace are always evident, making it easy to be transparent. Thank you for believing in me from the very beginning and pushing me to keep writing, moving me forward.

To my neighbor and friend, Jeanni Hommerding, you recognized my voice and how that needed to be consistent within my manuscript. Thank you for your availability, your faith, for loving and praying for my son, Corey, and for speaking truth, even when it is hard to hear.

To Tom Matlock, my favorite Bible scholar, who led me back to finding the inspiration within Scripture when I was at my lowest. The gift of God's Word and its application never became more important to me than when I needed to be comforted in grief and hear God's promises.

To Temple Scott, educator, leader, and co-worker, you encouraged me to speak boldly and tell of God's grace without reservation. Eternity is a long time. If I am telling my story, it is for the reader to know and seek the same grace upon amazing grace as well.

Last but not least, to my music minister, Robbie Cheuvront, you challenged me to tell you more, thus the first five chapters were added to the original manuscript when I thought I was finished. Now I can't imagine this story without those introductory windows and life-changing circumstances leading to the rest of the book. Those glimpses of life, love, and the wind-blown gathering of grace in the timeline, marked points of both joy and tragedy, and makes the grace even more amazing to me.

~~~

To those who helped get this book published, I am eternally grateful. My adult Sunday school class, Potter's House, for impromptu fundraisers during a pandemic, for checks in the mailbox, for friends across the United States buying my painted rocks and sending me payment for quadruple the price! I am overwhelmed with your generous love for me and your excitement to see this labor of love published.

Thank you to Nicole Liebgott for your photography skills and love.

Thank you Erik Sahakian and the Abundant Harvest Publishing team for believing in me from our very first conversation and telling me you felt this to be ordained. I believe that God gives grace upon grace and we are not to keep it, but send it out to the four corners of the earth, to tell of His glory and His wonders, His unfailing love and His healing in our deepest of despairs.

"Just when the caterpillar thought the world was over, it became a butterfly."

About the Author

Coleene VanTilburg discovered writing to be a catalyst to healing and connecting honestly with God. When she began sharing and trusting the Lord with her words, He orchestrated a ministry.

In 2009, with her friend and writing mentor, Linda Boutin, they started the Aspiring Writers' Forum, a group fellowship for writers at their home church in California's Chino Valley. Together, they have pursued small publishing opportunities in magazines and anthologies, as well as helping others with their writing projects and hosting community writers' conferences.

Coleene writes two blogs, *Friday Footnotes* (happy10toes.blogspot.com) and *Considerable Thoughts* (blogforeternity.blogspot.com).

She enjoys artistic endeavors, recently getting involved with painting rocks as well as gardening and listening to music.

Coleene, her husband, Ted, and their adult son, Corey, enjoy the outdoors and great times with family and friends.